ST. CLAIR:
I'll Take It Raw!

National Football League great and Pro Football Hall of Fame member Bob St. Clair

Kristine Setting Clark

Edited by Lorrie Aguirre-Laurence

Edited by Lorrie Aguirre-Laurence
Cover design by Robert Schnitzer
Front cover photo by San Francisco 49ers photo file
Back cover photo by Robert Schnitzer
ISBN # 0-9771765-0-9
First printing August 2005
Printed in USA by DeHart's Printing Services

How to order: *

Kristine Setting Clark
6 Saint John Court
Novato, California 94947

*Quantity discounts are available from the publisher

E-Mail: **khrystyne9@aol.com**

On your letterhead, please include information
concerning the intended use of books and the number of
book you wish to purchase.

ACKNOWLEDGEMENTS

I would like to thank Steve Sabol and Kathy Davis of NFL Films for their continued support and dedication to my projects.

I would also like to thank Ann St. Clair and Rosemary St. Clair-Umland for their wonderful stories and photos.

Thanks also to Rob Schnitzer for assistance with photos and layout without which this book would not be possible.

And as always, I would like to thank my editor, Lorrie Aguirre-Laurence for making this project a reality.

And last, but surely not least, to all those football players from football's Golden Era who honored me with their interviews.

To my dad, John Setting who took me to my first 49er game in 1958 and instilled in me the loyalty and pride of being a 49er Faithful.

FOREWORD

The first time that I saw Bob St. Clair was on the practice field at the University of San Francisco. I was very impressed by his size – 6' 8", 235 pounds. He looked more like a basketball player than a football player, which made me wonder whether or not he would succeed in the sport of football. It didn't take me long to find out!

One day our line coach, Bud Kerr, was running a drill on the far end of the field. Our team referred to this drill as "The Pit". Coach Kerr had anchored two dummies to the ground – each spaced three feet apart. When it was my turn to enter the pit my opponent was none other than Bob St. Clair. On the command of the coach we attacked each other like gladiators. Bob tried to keep me from penetrating his territory. He was incredibly strong and extremely aggressive. It was a tough fight and I think I may have won that first encounter, but I knew he would become a formidable opponent!

In 1952 I graduated from USF. The University's '51 football season was to be its last. Bob transferred to Tulsa University to complete his senior year and to play his final year of college football. At that point I had lost contact with him.

In 1953 Bob was drafted by the 49ers and I was a defensive end with the Baltimore Colts. When the Colts played the 49ers, I learned that the starting offensive tackle would be Bob. Prior to the game I was nervous and couldn't sleep. I knew what a tough guy he would be!

As we warmed up I tried not to have eye contact with him or talk with him because I considered him to be the "enemy". We battered each other "tooth and nail" throughout the entire game. When he held me I would cuss him out. It was a real battle and I can't say who won! When the game was over, we shook hands and walked off the field as friends once more.

In the years to follow we would face each other many times. Of all the offensive tackles that I had played against throughout my pro career, I can honestly say that Bob St. Clair was the finest of them all.

On a personal note, I count Bob not only as a college teammate and as an NFL opponent but as a true and valued friend.

Gino Marchett

"I'll take it raw!"

Contents

Photography Credits

FIRST QUARTER

A Hooligan From The City

Bob and his sister Rosemary, 1932

I was born, Robert Bruce St. Clair at home on February 18, 1931. The only thing they could weigh me on was a ten-pound scale that my mother kept in the kitchen. I weighed much more than that. Neither my mother, at 5'3', nor my father, at 5' 10', was particularly large. I, myself, was of average height and weight as a youngster.

My only sibling is my sister Rosemary who is 18 months my senior. She was always watching out for her 'baby' brother who seldom took heed to her warnings or advice.

When I was just 7 or 8 years old I had a bad habit of picking fights with boys that were 12 or 13 years old. Of course the boys used to beat me up so Rosemary would have to find them and beat them up! But when she got home, she would beat me for acting like such an idiot!

In the next few pages, Rosemary describes 'life with me'. Her first story takes place in the late 1930's.

A LITTLE GREEN

It was a warm summer evening. I was outside playing kick the can with some neighborhood kids. Bob was up the corner with his friends. It was time for us to go in, so I called to my brother to let him know.

Here he was coming down the street with a group of guys puffing on a cigar. He was only 6 or 7 years old at the time. I told him he was going to get sick and if Dad or Mom found out, he would really be in trouble. He continued to show off for his friends then threw the cigar away.

We began to walk home. All of sudden he got really sick. I got him into bed without our parents finding out what had happened. I remember laughing at him because he looked a little green. He didn't think it was very funny but I sure did. It would be a long time before he smoked another cigar.

THE FLAGPOLE

It was during the Depression. Both of our parents worked. We used to either play heats, kick the can or baseball in the street or in the schoolyard. When we played baseball, I would get picked before my brother. He wasn't very good then either.

One day he was flying a kite in the Farragut schoolyard.

Bob was about 10 years old then. He was running backwards while

watching his kite fly high up in the air. As he began to run faster, he

slammed the back of his head into the flagpole. There was a bolt that

was protruding from the poll and it went directly into his head. Since

my parents were both at work, I had to rush him home and take care

of him.

ROUGH TIMES – RAW MEAT

Our father, Bobby and I would be in the kitchen. Times were

hard back then. But every so often we would have meat. Our father

would be cooking and would say, 'Do you want a piece of meat?' He

would cut off a piece of that raw meat and salt it and we would have

a feast! We loved it! Both my brother and I eat raw meat to this day.

Early in life I learned about sports on the playground at
Farragut Elementary School. One day, while playing in a
neighborhood pickup game of football, one of the older kids broke
my nose. It was at that moment that I had decided that football
wasn't for me and made the decision to concentrate on a sport
somewhat less physically damaging like baseball or basketball. That
idea was short lived.

4

In the early 40's Rosemary and I and some of our friends were playing in the schoolyard across the street from their house. After a while, one of the guys and I decided to take our baseball bats and just for kicks, broke every single window on the first floor of the school. Rosemary thought my friends and are were crazy.

Why they did this I will never know. They didn't get caught.

I guess they were lucky. In those days, you never told on anyone.

You didn't want to be labeled a 'snitch'.

It is a wonder he grew up to be the somewhat normal, kind,

human being that he

is today.

THE DISAPPEARING HEARTS

It was around Valentines Day. Bob and I used to buy those small, cinnamon candy red hearts. One day we were in the car with my parents and he said, 'Hey Rose, I put a couple of those red hearts in my ear and they disappeared. See if you can put some more in.' I told him, 'OK, but you had better not tell mom or dad or I will beat you up!' He said, 'I won't, I won't.'

So here we are in the car going along when all of a sudden he starts crying and moaning. My mother, who was sitting in the front seat of the car, turned around and saw this red stuff coming out

of Bob's ear. She started screaming frantically, 'What's the matter?!

What's the matter?! Then she looked at me and said, 'What did you

do to him!' I yelled, 'I didn't do anything!'

My dad drove directly to the pharmacy where, at that time,

the pharmacist also doubled as a doctor. My dad grabbed my

brother and rushed him inside the pharmacy. The doctor looked at

Bob's ear and removed the candy hearts.

They both returned to the car and my dad told my mom what

had happened. When we got home, guess who got the beating?! I

had already warned my brother that I would get him if he told on me.

The next day I beat the shit out of him!

SCHOOL DAZE

Every Friday while sitting in class (in grammar school)), I

would get a call to go down to the office to pick up all the referrals

that my brother had received that week for being bad. He was

supposed to bring them home to mom and dad to sign; but instead he

threw them away. I used to hate going down to the office. I had to

bring a note home every Friday about his behavior. He was always

so bad. I could have killed him for that. Most of the time he would

6

make up great excuses and he got away with a lot. My brother

really thought he was 'hot stuff' when he was a kid – but I knew

better.

A POMPADOUR AND AN EISENHOWER JACKET

My brother was very conceited, especially during his

teenage years. Bob used to wear, what was called in those days, an

Eisenhower jacket. He wore his hair in a big pompadour, and

couldn't pass a mirror without combing it. He thought he was so

cool. I have to admit, he did look good. He's my brother and I love

him, but at times, he can be such a jackass.

When Bob was old enough to drive, my father let him use

the car on Sunday. He told them that he was going to church but

instead he would drive the car around and around the church. I

could hear the engine revving up each time he drove by.

In those days my father had a 1937 Chevy. Our house

didn't have a garage so he rented one up the street. One night Bob

had taken the car out for a joy ride (without permission) and was in

the process of putting the car back in the garage when my father

caught him. My father beat the hell out of him!

Like all brothers and sisters, Bob and I have had our share of ups and downs, good and bad; but through it all he's always been my baby brother - my best friend. I love him dearly and always will.

The year was 1941. I was 10 years old and I quickly learned the consequences of stealing – the hard way.

VEGETABLES AND ROCK SALT

My friends and I used to ride our bikes to the old farming areas where San Francisco State College now stands. The farmers would grow tomatoes, carrots, potatoes and other vegetables. We would jump the fences and steal the vegetables.

One day I jumped over the fence and went way out into the field. My buddy, Eddie screamed, 'Here comes the farmer!' I turned around to see that the farmer was coming at me with his truck. I ran into the field (where I knew he wouldn't drive in) and finally made it out to my bike. When I started peddling away I heard two explosions. All of a sudden I felt a stinging sensation in my butt and down my leg. The adrenalin was pumping and all I could think about was getting away.

I finally stopped and met up with the other guys. They said, 'Geez, Bob what happened? Did you fall down? You're bleeding all over the place!' I looked at my leg and said, 'Holy Christ!' There was rock salt imbedded in my leg and butt. It wasn't very deep but it sure burned like hell.

I went home and had my sister, Rosemary take it out. Needless to say I didn't go out stealing vegetables anymore.

FIRE!

When I was about 10 or 11 years old, I was walking with a so-called buddy of mine on Ocean Avenue. There was a big field on Ocean near City College. He was smoking. We were trying to be big shots. He handed the cigarette to me but I gave it back to him. We were across the street from the Prospect Bar on Ocean.

The cigarette had burned down and he flicked it into a field. The field had this tall grass that was about three feet high. We had just passed the grassy area when all of a sudden we smelled smoke. We turned around to see that the entire field had caught fire!

I ran across the street and broke the glass on the fire alarm. The fire department arrived and extinguished the fire. The police came over to us and asked if we had seen how the fire had started. I told him that I didn't know – that we were just walking by. One of the patrons from the Prospect Bar ran outside. He told the police that he saw the two of us walk by and throw a cigarette into the field. On that account, the police took my buddy and me to Juvenile Hall. It just so happened that my scoutmaster was a juvenile counselor at the Hall.

They separated my friend and me into two rooms. The scoutmaster came into my room. As soon as he saw it was me, he started reading me the riot act. I kept saying that I didn't do it because I didn't want to rat on my buddy. He kept telling me, 'You will never make anything out of your life. You are a troublemaker! You will end up being institutionalized!' Finally, the other counselor (who was with my buddy) came in and said, 'Your friend said that you started the fire.' I said, 'He's lying! He was the one with the cigarette - not me!' My parents had to come down to bail me out.

A BLACK EYE FOR THE BOY SCOUTS

When I was a boy scout we used to have our meetings in the basement of a church on Ocean Avenue near Miramar and Granada. It was close to my house on Capitol. As soon as we got out of the meeting, we used to all run down to the soda fountain on the corner of Miramar. It was one of those old-fashioned soda fountains.

One evening, for some reason, I was late in getting there. All the guys got there ahead of me and had taken all of the stools at the fountain area.

When I walked in one of the guys, who was a friend of mine, was drinking a soda from a straw. He sucked some soda into his straw then blew it at me as I walked by. I grabbed him and we began wrestling in the store. All of a sudden someone grabbed me by the back of the neck of my shirt and started pulling me down towards the door. He was yelling and screaming, 'You're a troublemaker! I want you out of here.' I didn't know who it was, but he had practically choked me with my Boy Scout scarf that was around my neck.

I knocked his arm away. He tried to grab me again, but this time I whacked him in the mouth and he fell back and crashed into the candy display. The candy went all over the floor. I ran out of there as fast as I could and went home.

I knew I was in trouble, so I didn't go directly into the house. We had a big chicken coup in the back (of the house) that was as high as the roof. I ran to the back so no one could see me, climbed up on top of the chicken coup and hid there. Sure as hell, here came the police to talk to my parents. I stayed there until they left. I then snuck into the back window of the house, where my bedroom was, and got into bed. That's when my mother came in screaming at me, 'The police were here!' My father followed her in screaming, 'We are going to be sued! The druggist had to go to the doctor and we have to pay the doctor's bill and the store bill.'

My father eventually worked it out with the druggist. But the scoutmaster was not too pleased with me. He said that this, along with the fire incident, proved that I was a menace. He told me to get the hell out of the troop.

Years later (when I was with the 49ers) I received a phone call from this same scoutmaster telling me that I *exemplified* what scouting is all about and that he would like for me to come down and talk to his troop. To prove a point, I went ahead and did it. I just found the whole situation so ironic!

GANG RIVELRY

In my youth on the streets of the Ingleside district in San Francisco, I ran with a gang of chain swinging, knife flashing, trouble-making punks who spent their more sociable moments at war with other gangs. Worse yet, some of the boys ended up in jail.

When I was 14 years old I was about 5' 9' and weighed around 150 pounds. One night I found out there was a party going on near Mission Street. By then we had moved to the Aptos area, which was on the other side of town. A couple of friends and I decided to crash the party.

There weren't too many guys at the party, but there were a lot of girls. After we were there for a while, we started making out with the girls. All of a sudden I saw a group of the 'pretty boy' guys, who were a little older than us, begin to gather around. I told my guys to get out – now - while they could. They all got away, but I stayed back. Being that I was the leader of the group, I waited to make sure that they all got out. I finally made my way out, but the 'pretty boy' guys ganged up on me. They lined up and started whacking me. I could clearly remember certain guys that were involved in this. When they finally took off, I ended up with a broken nose, a cracked tooth and cracked ribs. I was determined that I would get in shape and get these guys back. At that time, my father was taking a Charles Atlas course. For one year I physically worked my ass off. Within that year I grew 6 inches and put on 60 pounds.

One night while on my way to the show, I saw one of the guys who had beaten me up sitting in a booth at the soda fountain. I walked up to him, but he didn't recognize me. I said, 'Hey, remember me?' He was sitting with some girl. He said with a smirk, 'No.' I grabbed him by his shirt, slammed his head back into the back of the booth and said, 'You son of a bitch! I was the kid you and your friends held when you beat the shit out of me.' I whacked him with a right and backhanded him, breaking his nose. The girl started screaming. The manager came running over and I ran out.

Later I found out where one of the other gang members lived. He lived in the Mission District in one of those old flats where you 'turned' the doorbell to ring it. He was on the ground level. My friend and I had driven over in a 1938 Buick sedan. My friend kept the engine running while I rang the doorbell.

The gang member's mother came to the door. I asked her nicely if her son was there. 'Oh, just a minute.' she said. 'One of your friends is here.' He walked out and looked at me. I said, 'Remember me?' Before he could answer, I grabbed him and whacked him all the way down the hallway. His mother was screaming and yelling at me to stop. I ran down the steps, jumped into the car and we took off like the Green Hornet.

Word got out that 'you had better watch out for that guy'…meaning me.

A STREETCAR NAMED DISASTER

One night a group of us guys (we were teenagers) had some .22 caliber shells. We took the shells and placed them on the streetcar tracks on the corner of 19[the] Avenue and Taraval Street. When the streetcar would run over them, the shells would fire in all directions.

I was standing in front of the Parkside Theatre - down the corner from 19th when the next streetcar came by. The guys were putting the next set of shells on the track. As the streetcar came by, I jumped back into the doorway near the theatre. The shells went off. I came out and I was laughing; everyone was laughing. All of a sudden someone yelled, 'Watch out!' I turned around to find one of the streetcar conductors standing right behind me. I turned back around to run, and he swung this crowbar (switch bar) that hit me right on the side of the temple near my eye and knocked me flat as a pancake. I jumped up and couldn't see very well, but I took off running down the street anyway.

A couple of friends of mine met me; but by this time, my eye was completely shut. My head was swollen and my other eye was now beginning to close. The only way I could see was to 'physically' hold my eye open with my fingers.

We walked down from 19[the] Avenue to 35th Avenue. I knew there was a streetcar stop there and that that bastard would be returning. We had passed some construction sights along the way and I picked up one of the bricks that were lying there.

When we arrived at 35th, we hid in the bushes and waited for the son of a bitch to show up. I had to rely on my friends to tell me which conductor it was because I couldn't see very well at this point. We waited over an hour for him to return. Finally, he showed up.

'That's the guy, Bob!' my friend shouted. I ran out in front of the car and threw the brick, 'point blank', in front of the streetcar. When the conductor jumped out of the car, I whacked him then took off running.

I was crouched down under a tree when a squad car came by and picked me up. I was bleeding badly. They took me to the emergency. The x-rays showed that the conductor had cracked my skull.

After the doctor's had wrapped my head, I was taken to the police station. Naturally, the police phoned my parents and they had to come and pick me up.

At that time Pat Brown was the San Francisco District Attorney. My parents and I had to meet with him in his office with the conductor and his attorney. The conductor had bandages all over his face and a big black eye. My head was wrapped in bandages.

The conductor was going to sue my parents and my parents were going to sue him. It was a big mess. After hearing out both parties, Pat Brown dropped both sides of the suit.

Some of the boys eventually ended up in jail. They were picked up for 'petty' things. You know, like armed robbery - or a little trouble with the Interstate Commerce Commission – taking a stolen car across the state lines.

In fact many years later, we had a reunion of sorts. One year when I was with the 49ers, owner Franklin Mieuli got Joe Perry and I to go to San Quentin for the Olympic Games that they had over there. We were there to give a word of encouragement to the athlete prisoners. As we were walking through the main yard with all the prisoners around I kept stopping to talk to different people that I had known from the neighborhood. I had wondered where they had all disappeared.

When we got to the other side of the yard Franklin said, 'It's almost a tie between you and Perry as to how many guys here at Quentin you know from your old neighborhoods!

As a 5'9', 150- pound sophomore, Poly coach Joe Verducci told me that I was too small to play football. At the start of my junior season in 1947, I reported to Verducci at 6' 4', 210 pounds. Not only did I make the team but I made an impression on a young girl by the name of Ann Wickstrom.

AN ORCHARD, A JACKPOT AND A FIFTY-CENT RING

Bob was 17 years old and a senior at Poly. I was a freshman at City College. We had decided we wanted to get married. We also began to realize that Bob had a future in football as far as going to college; but to wait four years until he had graduated would be ridiculous. We decided to elope and keep it a secret.

I went to Woolworth's, across the street from where I worked, and bought a ring for fifty-cents. Of course it was glass. It wasn't even a good replica of a wedding ring.

Since neither of us had ever flown before, I decided that I would be the one to purchase the two tickets to Reno. But I was so naïve, that when I filled out the flight information, I give my 'home' phone number as a contact.

It was the morning of September 9th, Admission Day. Bob had the day off at school (at Polytechnic High) and I had the day off at work. I had told my mother that even though it was a holiday, I had to report to work very early that morning.

It was a very cold and foggy that day. I went to meet Bob at 19th Avenue and Taraval Street to catch the streetcar to go downtown. In those days you went back to the ticket agency where the tickets were purchased and then the agency bussed you to the airport. Well, the fog had become so thick that the airlines called my home to tell me that the flight had been cancelled. Instead, my mother answered the phone. 'What flight? What are you talking about?' she asked. And they told her. She frantically told them, 'They cannot go! Cancel those tickets!'

She threw on her bathrobe and ran down the street to see if she could catch me in time. But the streetcar had already come and she had missed us. My poor mother. I can only imagine what was going on in her mind. She must have been a wreck!

We finally arrived at the terminal. When we went to the ticket counter they told us that my mother said that we were not to go. So I called my mother and I told her that I had purposely not told her about the flight because I didn't want to worry her. I told her that we weren't going to Reno, but that we were going to Truckee and we would be back that night. She said it would be OK. So off we went....to Reno.

When we arrived in Reno, Bob bought me a corsage. We then went to the courthouse to get a license. They asked Bob how old he was and he said, ' Seventeen.' You were supposed to be eighteen, but in those days, no one asked for any identification. I guess it was because of his size that they didn't question him.

They charged us fifteen dollars for the license. We were on a tight budget. We thought the license was going to be five dollars. So consequently, we were now over budget.

We were now standing in front of the judge, when we realized that we didn't have any witnesses. The judge asked the janitor, who was mopping the courtroom floor, to be our witness. He leaned on his mop as we said our vows. The judge's secretary was our other witness. The cost of the ceremony was supposed to be fifteen-dollars but it turned out to be twenty-five dollars because he gave each witness five dollars!

We had planned to return to San Francisco by bus, but we only had enough money left for one fare. Bob decided to put me on the bus and he would hitch hike home. After paying for a ticket for me, he had a couple of dollars left. He put them in one of the slot machines and won ten dollars! Now we had enough money for both tickets. I had two 'cab tickets' in my purse - so when we arrived in San Francisco we at least had cab fare home.

We sat in the back of the bus. I had on my orchard and my $.50 wedding ring. The people on the bus stared at us knowing we were newlyweds. They even asked to see my ring! We stopped at one of the bus stops and Bob and I split a hamburger. It's all we could afford.

When we got home my mother was so grateful to see me. Sylvia, a friend of hers, was at the house. We told them both how much fun the plane ride was. What we didn't know was that Sylvia knew there wasn't an airport in Truckee.

And again, we were so dumb, that when the minister asked for Bob's address, he gave them his 'home' address. Sure enough, they sent the wedding certificate to his parents' home. It was addressed to Mr. and Mrs. Robert St. Clair. His father was also

Robert St. Clair. They opened up the letter and were shocked to

learn that the Mr. And Mrs. Robert St. Clair was not them, but their

son and his new bride. They never told my mom about the marriage.

They didn't even tell us that they knew! They kept it to themselves.

Soon after, I found out that I was pregnant. We had no

choice but to tell both my mother and Bob's parents that we would

soon be married in the church. And we would soon be waiting for a

new baby and a new football season.

THE CLOTHES LINE PLAY

In my senior year we were in the playoffs at Kezar Stadium

against Mission High. In my three years at Poly we had never lost a

game. We were going for a third straight championship.

Mission High's star back, Joe 'Scooter' Scudero, who I later

played with at USF, was really good.

It was the first quarter and Poly had just scored. We kicked

off and Joe caught the ball on the 20. He began to run the ball back

down the field. He tried to fake me out, and as he ran by, I clothes

lined him with a fist right to the face. I knocked him upside down.

His eye was all puffed up. Coach Schwartz, the Mission coach, chased me all over the field.

Throughout the rest of the game Joe's eye was shut. He couldn't see out of that one eye. When he ran with the ball he had to hold his eye open with the other hand. Of course, it made him ineffective.

As we came out of the tunnel in the second half, Scudero, holding his eye open, took a swing at me and missed. Naturally his missed. He was a foot shorter than me. I just pushed him away and ran out onto the field. Needless to say, we won the game. A year later, we were teammates at USF and became the best of friends.

Bob's exceptional performance at Poly earned him the title of All City tackle and a football scholarship to the University of San Francisco.

Bob's parents, Agnes and Robert St. Clair 1928

Bob, Agnes, Rosemary 1932

Rosemary, Robert, Bob 1942

Rosemary and Bob 1941

25

Bob and Fluffy

Rosemary and Bob 1940

Robert, Bob, Agnes, and Rosemary 1943

Cub Scout Troop
1941

The Family and Uncle Ed 1946

Members of the Polytechnic High Varsity Squad 1948
Rich Jones, Hal Goldstein, Bob, Marv Crews

Quarterback Dick Ellis (#32) and Bob at Kezar Stadium 1948

Polytechnic High Varsity End 1948

High School Graduation 1948

Bob and his wife Ann at a dance at City College of San Francisco
1948

SECOND QUARTER

Real Men Don't Wear Face Masks

Senior Year at University of Tulsa 1952

St. Clair was a product of the times - created by an era of crew cuts, two-way players and helmets without facemasks. In 1949 he won a scholarship to the University of San Francisco.

USF was a small Jesuit college bragging that its campus was 'The City' and its home field was Kezar Stadium (which also fielded SF high schools and the San Francisco Forty Niners). The team's training/equipment room at the University was a left over Quonset hut from World War II and both the football and baseball teams shared the same practice field.

But by 1951 the USF Dons were loaded with some of the finest talent in the nation and went undefeated and untied. Bob was selected for All Coast honors.

From 1948 through 1951, a culmination of four years as head coach, Joe Kuharich ('38 Notre Dame All-American) had molded a team that would send nine players to the NFL – three destined for the Pro Football Hall of Fame.

He conditioned his team both mentally and physically to outplay anyone. Joe's motto regarding the law of collegiate football was 'Produce or get out! And he meant it. They didn't call him 'the

Barracuda' for nothing. Bob's teammate, quarterback Bill Henneberry had this to say about Coach Joe.

We nicknamed Coach Kuharich 'The Barracuda' because if he wasn't happy with your performance, he would let you and the entire team know about it. He didn't talk a lot but when he did, the grass stood on end!

At a time when most college coaches were moving their spring practices to cooler environments, Coach Joe Kuharich was scanning the countryside in pursuit of a desolate, hot weather, summer training facility for his intensive two-week conditioning program for his players. His gridiron style of football literally came from the school of hard knocks. In August of 1950 he found his ideal in the remote town of Corning, California. The grueling workouts in the 115-degree heat combined with Kuharich's passion for 'old school' fundamentals and conditioning would prevail in the minds of his players for more than fifty years.

CORNING – HELL'S WRATH

Don's tackle, Gino Marchetti had this to say about training in the town of Corning.

When I think of Corning I think of being in the middle of a desert with no water and a little man yelling at you for six hours a day. Without a doubt, those were the roughest two weeks of my career. He treated everyone like a dog. But I guarantee you there was not a team in the country in better shape than we were

Bob thought that the coach's training methods were a little too 'extreme'.

Corning was Hell and Joe's work ethic was insane! There was nothing there except the field. No trees, no buildings, no shade. There was one telephone pole. If we'd get even a few minutes' break, ten guys would line up single file to get the shade from that pole. Joe Scudero (5'9') was the smartest guy on our team; he'd line up behind me (6'8').

That was my first real introduction to football the way it was done in the Midwest. It was so damn hot out there, you really had to dig down deep and pull on whatever guts you had.

I remember our first game after coming back from Corning. It was a night game at Kezar Stadium against Tulsa. They were one of the highest scoring teams in the nation the year before and they were favored by two touchdowns. But we tore them up physically. Little, rinky-dink USF cleaned their clocks.

Vince Tringali, one of our linemen (and like quarterback Ed Brown), was one of the craziest guys on the team. A man before his time – but I won't get into that. He figured the only way out of the torture was to leave practice and the only way to do that was to get knocked out. He had a plan that he was going to knock himself out. He started running into people and hitting the hell out of them. He got really dizzy, but unfortunately was unable to knock himself out. The guys even started complimenting him on all his good hits. Vince said,' Forget the hits, damn it, I wanna get knocked out!'

THE PIT

In order to keep your name on the roster, players would have to endure Kuharich's tortuous training methods. One of the more brutal drills took place in what we called The Pit. This was designed by Kuharich, himself.

He set up a couple of lightly padded railroad ties. Once the ties were in place players were forced to squeeze between them and battle each other one on one - gladiator style. You'd hit, scratch and bite– anything to get through. There were some real fistfights in there.

Every time Tringali had to go up against myself or Marchetti in the Pit, he would fake tying his shoe and tell the next guy to go in front of him.

Corning and the Pit personified Joe's work ethic. We became the leanest, meanest, best-conditioned football machine that maybe ever played the game. We knew we could beat any team in the country

ALONG THE WAY

The game I remember as my most physical was when we played St. Mary's. I'd caught a pass, faked out a defender and was running full blast down the sidelines. I saw a defensive back coming along the goal line, and I thought I'd charge right through him. The next thing I knew, he went under my legs, I went right up in the air and when I came down, it almost knocked me out. I couldn't walk because of a charley horse. The guy who hit me was future 49er teammate and Hall of Fame member, John Henry Johnson.

THE DREAM TEAM – '51 DONS

After the '51 season, Coach Kuharich made the statement, 'If that team had Notre Dame on their jerseys, they would have built a monument in their memory.'

Pete Rozelle who was our athletic publicist at USF and who later went on to be NFL Commissioner said, ''If I could start an NFL franchise with just that team I really believe that in two to three years we would have been champions.

Looking back, it was the best decision I had ever made. USF gave me a strong educational foundation that molded the values I hold to this day. It also gave me the opportunity to play football on the single greatest collegiate football team ever assembled. It was my great fortune to have played with such a unique group of gifted athletes. Our 1951 undefeated and untied team speaks for itself. The camaraderie we shared on and off the field extended far beyond that of Kezar Stadium. We shared a common goal – to be better than we imagined possible; to be over-achievers not only on the playing field but academically and in life.

THE FINAL GUN

The '51 team went undefeated and untied that year. A perfect 9-0 season but they were denied an Orange Bowl bid because they had two Black players on the team Ollie Matson and Burl Toler. The team had a chance to go without the Black players. They adamantly refused. Losing the bowl bid cost the team the revenue they needed to continue the program. The '51 season was to be the final football season for the Dons of USF.

TULSA

With the University's decision to discontinue football, I finished out my senior year at Tulsa University.

The Missouri Valley Conference that Tulsa played in didn't require transfers to sit out a year. so it was beneficial for me to finish up there. We had a hell of a year. I played well enough to be invited to the East-West Shrine Game back at Kezar and I was all excited to come back here. Then the next day the team got invited to play Florida in the Gator Bowl. When the Shrine Committee heard about that they sent me a Shrine Game watch.

It was at Tulsa that I met and T-KO'd the local Golden Gloves boxing champ in a bout that took 30 seconds to complete and 45 minutes to calm the unruly fans.

Later on that same year I also defeated a tornado. The fight was by far the easier of the two.

The boxing heavyweight division in northeastern Oklahoma was short of entrants, and the captain of Tulsa's football team suggested that I make an appearance. I agreed. Below is a blow-by-blow account of what really happened.

THE ORIGINAL 'ROCKY'

When USF abandoned football back in 1951, I was still only a junior and had one more year of eligibility left so the University of Tulsa asked me to come and play for them my senior year. I accepted. The reason I picked Tulsa rather than some of the other colleges that had inquired about me was that the Missouri Valley Conference was the only conference in the country at that time that would recognize a transfer without having to red shirt - .in other words, sit out a year. When I arrived I figured the football team would welcome me with open arms. And rightfully so. Here was an All-Coast coming to Tulsa to help them. But this turned out not to be the case. There was a great deal of animosity between the players and I. They were a pretty tight knit group. Here was a kid from the West Coast coming in to take one of their 'good ole boys' position. They gave me the cold shoulder.

About a week later, the captain of the football team said, 'Bob, we would like to have you do us a favor.' I said, 'What do you mean...me do you a favor?' 'This week in Tulsa is the Golden

Gloves' finals and we don't have a heavyweight to represent the University. We would really appreciate it if you would do it.' Well, wait a minute.... I don't know anything about fighting professionally. Yeah, I've done a lot of street fighting while growing up in San Francisco, but as far as getting in the ring with all those Queensbury Rules, I don't know a thing.' 'Don't worry about it, Bob. It's only three rounds and about three hundred people, and we'll be in your corner.

I thought about it and figured it might be a good way to get in with the guys. So I accepted. The night of the fight I took my valise. I didn't have any of the necessary equipment...only a red bathing suit, white socks and a pair of US Keds. I put them all in my bag and caught the bus. The boxing event was held at the Tulsa Civic Auditorium. When I walked into the auditorium, there were at least 5000 people there. It looked just like a scene out of the movie *Rocky*. The lights hung low over the ring and you could hear the murmur of the crowd.

I was escorted to the dressing room where the trainer told me to change and wait outside. So I put on my red bathing suit, socks, etc. He said, 'Wait a minute! Where's your robe?' I told him

I didn't have a robe so he gave me this kimono that fit me like a mini-skirt...at least it was red so it matched my trunks.

I stepped outside the room to watch the fights that were before me. The lightweight divisions went first. First round, Bam! Down goes the Tulsa bantamweight; next was the Tulsa welterweight - Bam! He goes down. Right down the line...they all got whacked in that first round. I thought to myself, 'Maybe I made a mistake on this one....poor judgment.' But I had to go through with it. So now it was my turn.

I walked down the aisle to the ring. They were laughing at how I was dressed. I took my robe off and jumped into the ring not knowing exactly what to do. I looked over to the corner and there, sitting ringside, were all the Tulsa football players drinking beer and having a good ole time. They were laughing and yelling, 'Hey champ....kill em!' Just then there was this huge roar from the crowd. Here came my opponent down the aisle...white towel around his neck, blue satin robe and on the back of the robe I noticed there were crossed golden gloves – that meant he was last year's state champion. He climbed into the ring and began to weave and bob. And then he did some knee bends. So I began to weave and bob and do some deep knee bends.

He goes over and kicks his feet around in the sand or whatever (I didn't know what the hell it was) and then I go over and kick my feet around. The bell rings and the referee has us come on out to the middle of the ring to get the instructions. I was so nervous that I never heard a word that he said. Not one word - except when he said, 'Go back to your respective corners and come out fighting.'

I went back to my corner and here were the guys....'go get em, killer!' (Ha, ha, ha). The bell rang and I walked out to the middle of the ring, as did my opponent. He put his two gloves out to touch gloves and I whacked him with a left and then a right. Well, everyone was booing and the referee was yelling and screaming at me. The touching of the gloves was one of the things that the referee had told me but I had never heard. I said, 'Ok, Ok.' And he said, 'Start fighting.'

We started dancing around and finally he threw a left and then I threw a left and our gloves hit head on. He backed up and I backed up. At that point (for some reason) I thought he was afraid of me. I didn't know. I went right after him right across the ring. He hit me numerous times. I didn't feel a god damn thing. As he did a fake, a bob and a move he went right by me and I grabbed him by the neck. I pushed him back into the corner. I whacked him with a left and then a right and he started to go down. I put my gloves under his armpits and lifted him up. I whacked him again. He went to the ground on his hands and knees. I hit him in the back, neck and head. Someone was pulling at my arm. I hit him. That was the referee. He went down. There was so much debris in the ring. The booing was deafening. I looked and the referee got up and picked up the white towel that my opponent's manager threw in. He threw in the white towel. I won by a TKO. The manager later said that he wasn't going to ever let his guy fight me. 'That guy's insane.', said the manager. 'He's goofy!' The only people in the auditorium who were clapping and cheering were the Tulsa football team.

The moral of the story is: I got in good with the guys.'

THE BLACK WALL AND OTHER FUN THINGS

We were having great luck, catching 'em like flies, when I looked down river and saw a big black cloud on the ground, headed towards me. It looked like a black wall. My friend who was approximately 100 yards away from me began screaming and waving at me hysterically. At the time was drizzling a little and the wind had started to whip. Finally I realized he was saying, 'Tornado!' We raced up the riverbank and piled into the car for protection just as the tornado struck full force.

The car was bouncing up and down. All four wheels were off the ground at times. Finally the wind picked up the car and hurled it against some cement bulkheads. The car stood upward leaning against the bulkheads – the wind banging it. The bulkheads probably saved our lives. Finally the tornado passed on.

Another time while I was duck hunting, I slipped face down underwater into a deep hole and found myself being sucked down into the mud. I was drowning AND suffocating. I began crawling through the muck to where I thought the shore to be. When I awoke, I was on the bank with only my head above water.

I especially remember a hunting trip that I went on with Tulsa lineman Floyd Harrawood. We had just bagged ourselves a deer. I immediately cut the deer's throat and drank the blood. He almost passed out!

The night before a game in Detroit, I summoned Tom Miner and our quarterback Tommy Hudspeth to accompany me to a food store where I ordered a pound of liver. When the butcher prepared to package the liver I said, 'I'll eat it here.' And I did! That butcher stood there with his mouth open, as did both of my teammates. I am not sure the butcher knew what to make of me

ST. CLAIR 'MISSING'
Big Tackle visiting New 'Little Tackle'
John H. Turner/Tulsa World sportswriter

Bob St. Clair, 6'7', 230 pound tackle figured to be one of the failed to appear for the regular practice session yesterday – and for a few minutes there was cause for alarm. But big Bob had a legitimate reason. At age 21 he became a father for the second time.

At 6:45 a.m. yesterday in St. John's hospital, the stork delivered a seven-pound, 14-ounce baby boy to the St. Clairs. He was named Gary Robert, and he looks like a prospective tackle or fullback, Bob thinks.

Mrs. St. Clair and Gary Robert were reported getting along splendidly last night, but Bob looked a little pale from the ordeal. He'll be back in harness tomorrow as the Hurricane reviews its drills.

The St. Clair's already have a daughter, Lynn, 2 years old.

RECEIVING THE CALL

In the spring of '53 I received a call from Pete Rozelle (at that time PR Director for the Los Angeles Rams). He told me that the Rams were looking at me and to hang tight. As it turned out Jon Arnett from USC was selected in the third round by LA. Before the

Rams could select again, I had already been drafted by the 49ers and would be returning to my hometown of San Francisco.

St. Clair would be best known in the National Football League for his size, speed, intelligence and his love of hitting. But it would be his 'flamboyant' lifestyle that made many stand up and take notice!

Front Row, L. to R.: Hillig, Tringali, Sachs, Weibel, Carley, Stephens, Thomas, Peacock, Henneberry, Dawson, Kearney. *2nd Row:* Trainer Frank Zanazzi, Whitney, Scudero, St. Clair, Matson, Marchetti, Toler, Brown, Mergen, Sakowski, Thiel, Manager Dick Domeno. *3rd Row:* Huxley, Boggan, Shaefter, Dwyer, McLaughlin, Slaichert, Madden, Montero, DeBernardi; *Back Row:* Monti, Dando, McMahon, Colombini, Bruna, Roland, Moriarity, Welsh.

The 9-0 University of San Francisco team of 1951

47

Bob and Ann holding Lynn, their first child

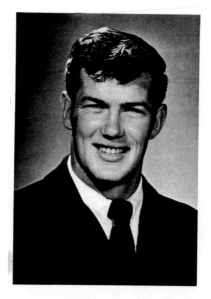

Bob during his junior year at USF 1950

The University of Tulsa Football Team 1952

Bob and Gary, his second child

Floyd and Bobbie Harawood with Ann and Bob at a U of Tulsa
dance 1952

Bob's Golden Gloves debut at Univ of Tulsa 1952

Bob says good bye to Ann and Lynn as he leaves for the Gator Bowl
1953

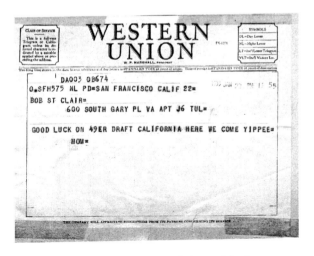

His mother telegrams Bob good luck

THIRD QUARTER

His Trademark:
Violence, Strength and Power

BOB ST. CLAIR   Tackle   6-9, 265

SAN FRANCISCO FORTY NINERS

1960 promotional photo

St. Clair's violence, strength and power left a trail of broken bones throughout the NFL. He wasn't just good – he was mean; a quality that led other players to salute him in a less than flattering manner.

For some of the players, St. Clair induced nightmares that linger to this day. One of those gridiron greats was Deacon Jones, defensive lineman for the Los Angeles Rams.

Although I have not played against Bob St. Clair since 1962, I still have nightmares about him.

THE LEAGUE'S FIRST HOLDOUT?

In 1953 I was a senior at Tulsa University in Oklahoma. I didn't think much about being drafted into the NFL. Then, one day, I received a call from University of San Francisco (where I began my college career) alumnus Pete Rozelle. Pete was now working for the Los Angeles Rams and told me that the team was interested in drafting me. Being a native of San Francisco I looked forward to getting back to the west coast. '

When draft day came around, I couldn't sit still. I was so nervous. Soon, the draft was into the third round and the Rams had not yet selected me. Pete called to tell me not to worry because they would grab me in the next round.

Before that could happen, I received a call from Tony Morabito, owner of the San Francisco 49ers. He had taken me in the 3rd round, 32nd pick overall. Morabito was so elated to a get hometown product that he offered me a $5,000 contract. The sum, as described by Morabito, was a little more than average for a rookie.

I told him, 'I'm sorry Mr. Morabito, but I need $6,000.' He immediately hung up on me.

A week later Tony called again and upped his offer to $5,000 and a $500 bonus if I were to make the team. I turned down his offer.

My reasoning for what has been described was perhaps the NFL's first holdout was that I knew my fellow Tulsa teammate Marv Matuszak had signed with the Green Bay Packers for $6,000.

I knew I was as good as him so I held firm on my demands. Fortunately we came to an agreement – and as they say, the rest is history.

Back in those days we would sign a blank contract then turn the contract over to Tony (Morabito) and let him write in the amount he thought was fair. He always told us that he would see to it that we were taken care of - and he always did.

Now Paul Brown, coach of the Chicago Bears, looked at players' salaries from a different prospective.

Many of these men had just returned from the service – a war.
This was a picnic compared to what they had been through – and it was a
privilege. You didn't have all of the high salaries and agents that you have
today. It was an extremely competitive, tough proposition, but when you
made it, it sure was a lot of fun.

A former teammate and good friend of mine, defensive lineman
Dan Colchico, tells how he responded to receiving his contract.

After signing the contract (not to say that the 49ers were cheap)
one of the team's administrators Lou Spadia would ask us not to discuss it
with anyone. 'Now remember Dan, don't discuss your contract with
anybody.' 'Don't worry, Lou. I'm just as ashamed of it as you are!'

In those days we weren't paid a dime during the first three weeks
of training camp. When the season began, we were paid only $50.00 a
game!

With today's salaries the right tackle makes two million dollars a
year. That is approximately $160,000 per game. I played a total of twelve
years for a total salary of $155,000. So the first game that this tackle plays,
he makes $5000 more than I did in twelve years. You think that pisses me
off!

MY ROOKIE SEASON

When I reported to the 49ers as a rookie in 1953 I immediately was matched one on one against Leo Nomellini. Leo was an al-pro defensive tackle on his way to one of the great durability records in sport – 266 consecutive football games – including preseason. Nomellini weighed 265 and was counted on to give me my initiation into the NFL.

Our confrontation has been described as 'a couple of bull elephants trying to get out of a telephone booth'. Lucky for me, I made the cut.

Leo had this to say about me making the team.

We were really struggling to find a tackle who could play offense. When we got Bob, the struggle was over. He fit right in with the team. He was really well received by the guys and everyone else, the coaches included! I was playing both ways at the time – offensive and defensive tackle so when Bob came to the 49ers, we had finally found a player that could secure the offensive tackle position. Now I only had to play the defensive tackle position which is what I wanted.

One of the major problems that we faced in those days was that there were only had about 33 or 35 players on a team. There wasn't room for good football players who actually could have made the team, but who weren't in the right place at the right time. We played everything. In my first three years, back in the '50s, I played both offense and defense – hardly left the field. And all the special teams – that was an automatic. So there really wasn't any room for a guy who could only do one thing. There was no room for specialists. No way!

We had to be innovative. I would fire out on a pass play just to try to fool them and then leg-whip like crazy. Leg whipping was legal in those days. Ask some of those guys I played against about leg whips. They thought they got by me and then – *whacko!* Down they would go. My heel would be hitting them right in the groin or in the chest. I used to put shin guards on backwards so I wouldn't hurt my calves.

We were handicapped by the way we had to block. We couldn't' use our hands the way they do now. I watch linemen block now with their arms spread out, and it's hard for me to believe that anyone could have gotten by me with my wingspread if I could have done that. I would have loved to play under those conditions.

The game is built around roughness. There is a personal thrill out of knocking a man down - really hitting him. It is the only satisfaction a lineman has. It gets you up. It gives you a jolt of the ol' adrenaline.

One of the things you have to understand about offensive linemen is that they have a continuous chip on their shoulder. They are always mad - either at the guy across the line or at the backs

behind them. The backs always get the glory when things go well

and the lineman take the guilty when things go wrong. No one

knows how important you are until you fail.

There were a few coaches in the NFL that felt that I was too

tall to be an effective football player. One of those men was Lisle

Blackbourne, coach of the Green Bay Packers.

Once during a game against the Packers Blackbourne

decided to test his theory. He sent Hawg Hanner and Gus Cifelli –

both 250 + pounds each – to hit me at the chest and ankles

simultaneously. Blackbourne thought that a hit like that would put

me right out of the game. Boy, was he wrong. Hanner drove in low,

but I smashed him in the face with my hand while Cifelli bounced

right off my chest. Blackbourne never again doubted my ability as a

football player.

During my rookie season we used to practice down in Menlo Park.

Everyday after practice we would have a meeting. In the afternoon I would

get so tired…it was so hot. One afternoon I was sitting by the window and I

was chewing Beechnut tobacco. Our coach Buck Shaw was talking to the

team. The sun was beating down on me from the window and I dozed off.

The first thing I heard when I came to was the coach's loud voice saying,

'Isn't that right St. Clair? Isn't that right?' He obviously caught me sleeping and it startled me. I jumped up and what happened was that I swallowed my tobacco…but it lodged in my throat. I began gagging and I couldn't answer him. He continued to ask, 'Isn't that right? Isn't that right?' He wanted to make an example of me for falling asleep. I ran out of the room to get outside and bent over on the lawn. I finally coughed it up. The guys inside later told me that the coach said, 'I don't know what's wrong with the kid. He might be somewhat of a mental case!'

Another good friend and teammate of mine, Hall of Fame member, Joe (The Jet) Perry fondly remembers a game that we played against the Browns in Cleveland during my rookie season.

I remember one time when we played the Browns at Cleveland. Bob, who was a rookie that year and Cleveland defensive tackle Don Joyce were really going at it. Punches began to fly on the first play from scrimmage. First Joyce punched Bob then Bob punched Joyce. The problem was that the referee only saw St. Clair throwing the punches (which was what Joyce wanted – a typical rookie mistake). The 49ers ended up with the penalty. Our coach, Buck Shaw was mad as hell at him!

49ER/EAGLES BRAWL

In 1953 we played a home game that produced a riot between the 49ers and the Philadelphia Eagles, who had had bad blood since the 49ers Charley Powell had started a fight in an exhibition game in Texas.

It was my rookie year. Hugh McElhenny was chasing Philadelphia Eagle Pete Pihos with his helmet (and eventually catching him and whacking him over the head). All hell broke loose. Both benches cleared. Everybody was fighting in the end zone. Fans were throwing bottles and cans. Joe McTeague, the 49er band leader, was trying to play *The Star Spangled Banner* to maybe restore some order, but guys were being thrown into the band and knocking the instruments off their stands.

ROOMING WITH Y.A.

49er quarterback, friend and future Hall of Fame member, Y. A. Tittle was my roommate during my rookie season. At training camp I couldn't sleep at night because Y would snore so badly. I was so tired during practice from lack of sleep that I was afraid of being cut. Tittle tells how I solved the problem.

Bob was my roommate with the 49ers in 1953. He was a good roommate...a lot of fun. He likes to tell this story. It's a true story. We called Bob, the vampire. When we would go on road trips you wouldn't see Bob during the day - only at night.

He was a fun loving guy. He ate raw liver, meat, chicken, and eggs. He ate everything raw. I would not have breakfast with him. He used to get mad at me. I couldn't eat anything while watching him eat a raw egg.

Anyway…. this story is true. I have asthma and I wheeze sometimes at nighttime. Bob being my roommate, we had twin beds in the room. We were at training camp. I would wheeze and he couldn't sleep. He was trying to make the team, as he tells it. He was a rookie and he was out to beat the competition. So he wants to make the team, and is living with a so-called star quarterback and he can't go to sleep. So he doesn't want to kick me out cause that would really be insulting and being my roommate, he thought would give him a little extra chance to make sure he would make the team. So one night he decided he was going to stop it.

I began wheezing with my asthma. He walked over to me and he kissed me on top of the head, patted my rear end and said, 'Good night, darlin'. And he got into bed. He slept like a baby all night long because I never wheezed one more wheeze because my eyes were open all night just staring at the ceiling. I wasn't sure as to what kind of roommate I had.

A MATTER OF COLOR

Sportswriter Mickey Herskowitz talks about the NFL and integration (or the lack of it) in the 50's.

But the fifties were not all candy for our soul. Integration was a new, uneasy word. The steps taken to erase the traces of the color line were small ones, and slow. But they also were the hardest and the most meaningful, because they were the first.

This story pertains to the Black situation in the south during the early 50's. With the exception of our USF team not playing in a bowl game because of our two black players, Ollie Matson and Burl Toler, I had not experienced this type of racism as a professional football player.

I was a rookie and we were flying into Baltimore to play the Colts. Joe Perry and I were very close friends. They were only a couple of us players who lived in San Francisco. Training camp was down in Menlo Park. Joe and I would drive down to training camp together in the morning. He would drive one week and I would drive the other. We were sitting next to each other in the plane and as we were getting ready to land in Baltimore I told Joe, 'Hey, listen. As soon as we register I'll give you a call and tell you which room I'm in and then we'll go out. You gotta know where all the action is in this town.' And he said, 'Well I'm not staying in the hotel.

I'll call you.' I said, 'What do you mean you're not staying in the hotel?' He said, 'Well, I'm staying in a private house.' I said, 'What? You lucky bastard. You get to stay in a house. I guess as a rookie I have to stay in a damn hotel! Hopefully, after a couple of years in the league I might be able to stay in a private house too!' Being from the West Coast that's how naive I was! He couldn't stay in a hotel because Blacks weren't allowed.

BEDCHECK

It was my second year with the team. We were playing Chicago and were staying at the Hotel Wyndamir East located in Hyde Park. Leo (Nomellini) and I had bed checks at about 11:00. I convenienced Leo to go downtown so we could *do up the town.* I said to him, 'You gotta show me where the action is!' So we went out to a couple of bars and had a few drinks. It's now about1:00 a.m. Leo said, 'We better get back to the hotel.' This was early in the week so it didn't affect practice.

We knew that once we arrived at the hotel we would have to sneak in the back so no one would see us coming through the front door. We were walking the walkway trails in the park towards the hotel. All of a sudden, this guy jumps from out of the bushes. He has a clipboard and a pen and says, 'Ok you guys, where have you been?' Leo says, 'We went to a late show.' 'Well I hope you enjoyed it because it's going to cost you!' Leo said, 'You little runt! I'm going to break your neck!' Leo began to chase the guy. It was Lou Spadia who later became the General Manager of the 49ers. Lou took one look at Leo and ran. I yelled to Leo, 'Leave him alone, we have to get to bed!'

The next morning we had a meeting with our coach, Buck Shaw. First thing he said when he came in was, 'I'm really disappointed in you guys. I have used the honor system with you guys my whole coaching career. I have never had a problem. But last night I was really concerned.' As he was talking I knew he was talking directly to me. I figured Spadia had told him that Leo and I were the two guys who were out. Being it was only my second year…. I was slumping down in my chair. Then he said, 'I can't believe it….how would your wives like to know you were out!' Now I'm really slumped down in my chair. Then he said, 'Last night out of 33 players 28 of you guys were out!' All of a sudden I sat up in the chair. I thought, 'Geez that's not too shabby.' He fined us all $50.00. We were playing the Bears that week. Later on he said that if we beat the Bears that week that he would disregard the fine. Not only did we beat them badly but we weren't favored either!

Another funny story happened while at training camp. I had been with the 49ers for quite a few years now and thought that I had seen it all. I was wrong.

One night after practice Dan Colchico and I decided to sneak out and go hunting. This rookie guard from Kansas named John wanted to go out hunting with us. He told us that he always hunted deer back in Kansas. He kept begging us and begging us, so finally we told him he could go.

Spotlighting at night was illegal. I had a brand new 1960 Cadillac convertible and we were driving it through the orchard. The spotlight was connected to the cigarette lighter. Dan was holding the light. We passed some cows and all of a sudden John said, 'There's one, there's one.' Dan said, 'Where, where?' John said, 'Go back, go back!' We backed up the car. 'See him right there?' said John. All Dan saw were some cows. Dan said, 'I don't see him, but if you see him, take him.'

Even though we had a scope on the rifle neither Dan nor I saw the deer. We thought that since John was an *experienced* hunter, he could spot them better than we could. All of a sudden the rifle exploded and we heard…Moo. 'You dumb son of a bitch. You shot a cow!' I said.

We ran over to the cow, tied him to the back of the car and towed him over to a ravine and dumped the carcass. We broke branches and trees and threw them into the ravine to cover the animal. We returned to training camp but didn't tell anyone what had happened.

The next day we were out on the field at practice doing jumping jacks. Dan said, 'Bob, Bob. Look over there!' Dan pointed to where the ravine was. There was nothing but buzzards circling around the area.

That night after dinner our coach Frankie Albert called a special meeting. At the meeting he introduced us to the sheriff of the county and the fish and game warden. 'These gentlemen are here because they found a dead cow in the ravine. It had been shot. Do any of you know anything about this or of anyone who may be carrying a rifle?' Frank knew that I carried a rifle and he kept looking at me the whole time he was talking. I turned to Dan and Ed (Henke) and said, 'Do any of you guys remember seeing anyone with a rifle?' They shook their heads. 'No, we didn't see anyone.' I said. Frankie looked right at the sheriff and fish and game warden and said, 'We don't allow any guns during training camp.'

After they left Frankie said, 'St. Clair, come here! Are you crazy? What happened?' I told him, 'Coach, John said he hunted before. How did I know he didn't know the difference between a cow and a deer?'

From that day on, guns were outlawed from training camp.

THE CONNOISSEUR

In my playing days my diet consisted of raw eggs, raw liver and various raw meats. When I would go out to eat I would tell the waiter to 'just take it out of the icebox and put it on the plate! At this time I had also acquired a taste for wheat germ oil, raw honey and beer, vodka screwdrivers and chewing tobacco. There were many players who wouldn't eat with me. They would get sick watching me eat raw meat – especially raw liver.

One time we were in a great restaurant in Minneapolis called *Charlie's*. Everyone was ordering these great dishes. I had asked the waiter to bring me some raw liver. He looked at me sarcastically and said, 'Raw liver? You've got to be kidding!' I stood up, looked down at him and said, 'I'm going to grab your skull with my hand and crush it like an eggshell. Get that liver out of the icebox now! Don't go near the grill – just bring it to the table!'

By this time everyone had begun to eat. Finally, the waiter showed up with my raw liver – with a small side of blood on the plate. He set it down in front of me and I immediately started slicing it up and eating it. The veterans on the team started laughing because they were all used to it. But some of the rookies made a quick exit, as did the woman at the table next to us.

Another time we (the team) were having lunch in Chicago. I wanted trout. The waiter brought me a trout but it was cooked. I didn't want a *cooked* trout. I wanted it taken out of the refrigerator and put on the plate. I made such a big deal about it that the people at the other tables started looking around. I guess they wanted to know what I was going to do with this trout.

Anyway, the waiter returned with an uncooked trout on my plate - the eye staring right at me. By now there were a lot of people staring at me wondering what I was going to do. I took the trout by the head, took my thumb and popped the eye out and caught it on my tongue. The whole place went nuts. I finished eating the trout.

During the season some of us would go dove hunting. One day I had about 12 or 15 doves. We were plucking them and cleaning them and I would take the hearts and make a little pile of dove hearts. This kid from Nebraska came over and said, 'What are you doing with that pile of hearts?' I answered that I was going to eat them. The kid asked me if I was going to make some kind of a sauce. I said. 'Sauce! No! You see these?' And then I put two in my mouth and started to chew on them. He turned three different colors. I thought he was going to faint right there. He ran out of the room. I'm sure he called home and said, 'There are cannibals out here!'

In 1961 we acquired a quarterback from UCLA by the name of Billy Kilmer. I took it upon myself to take Billy under my wing and introduce him to the finer points of life within NFL. This is what he had to say about his induction.

St. Clair made me feel that I was part of the team. After practice the veterans would get together and go out for a beer. The rookies went home.

One day as I was walking off the field (after practice) St. Clair stopped me and said, 'Hey rookie, why don't you come and have a beer with us. You've earned it.' At that point I knew I had been accepted by the team.

Bob was extremely debonair. Football players were usually sloppy, but Bob was always concerned about how he looked, dressed and acted. You'll never find a classier person. He taught me a lot about how you should handle yourself in public but he could never convenience me of his eating habits.

During training camp we would hunt for deer. Bob had a '62 Cadillac convertible. Everyone called it the Safari Wagon. After the meetings at night we would all get into the Cadillac and go looking for deer in the pear orchard. Here we were cruising in this Cadillac convertible in the pear orchard. One night we saw this deer running and I had this rifle in my hand. I wasn't that good of a shot and I stuck it right out right over these guys ears and shot this deer right in the head, and this deer was comin right at us and everyone was yellin get out of the way! The deer fell 10 feet from the car. If I hadn't shot it, it would have run right over us.

Bob would take the deer up to an old bar where they would skin the deer. Another guy would come in and he owned a cold storage locker ---he would cut the deer up in steaks and hamburger and the next day we would have the deer meat packaged and ready. But what Bob used to do is cut the liver out and put it in a towel – it was still warm from the carcass. And this was just before bed check. After bed check, I would sneak down to Bob's room for a couple of beers and here he is slicing off pieces of hot liver, the blood running down his hand, eating it right there and drinking a beer, and here was Tommy Davis, our kicker, leaning out the window throwing up. He couldn't stand it. It was really funny.

THE RECRUITS

Dan Colchico tells a great story of how he and I used to deal with the new recruits at training camp.

The 49ers would draft all these guys from back east. This was one of Bob's games that he devised. What we would do is get these guys to go out and have a beer with us. We would start drinking beer with ice so you wouldn't get bloated and you could sweat it out. So some of these guys would come in and ask for a shot. 'Give him another shot, we would say.' Because we knew that the next day at practice he was going to die. Hell, we loved it. Pretty soon we would be waving him good-bye because he was heaving. This was all part of Bob's plan. This was the second part of his plan. These guys would come here thinking they were going to take our positions. The first thing we have to tell them is how great it is to be on the West Coast right here at St. Mary's and you know, our wives are only a half hour away. He would ask them if they were married or did they have a girlfriend? Was she by herself, does she ever get lonely? Does she call you all the time? Ya know, it's nice for us because our women are only half an hour away and we can get in the car and go see them. A few minutes later you would hear the car engine rev up and they would be gone. 'Well, there goes another one!' One time they cut so many players that they had to cancel practice!

One year we had this guy who came to us from the hills of West Virginia. He was running down the road one day when two 49er scouts drove up beside him. They were looking at their speedometer while watching this guy run. He looked like Superman!

They brought him to camp. He was so chiseled that we nicknamed him Clark Kent, but we considered him Superman. His only problem was that he had very poor vision. It didn't seem to bother him because during the exhibition season Hickey would have him running down the field – full speed - on kickoffs... breaking up the wedge and smashing into the ball carrier. He was unbelievable. Hickey said that if he was that good, he would get contacts for him. 'He'll be a superstar!' he said.

The problems began the moment they gave him contacts. As he began running down he could now see what was in front of him and began 'tiptoeing through the tulips'. We laughed.

One day we were both working out at the Marines Memorial Gymnasium. We both had been hurt. He could lift twice as much weight as I could with his legs. He was a real weightlifter. He was working out on the leg press machine. There was about 500 pounds of weight already on the machine. He was lifting it like it was nothing. He kept asking me to put on more and more weight. There was a great deal of weight on the bar when he asked me to release the snaps to let the weight come down. He was trying to lift the massive amount of weight and was turning red as a tomato. The poor guy began choking. I yelled to the instructor to help me lift this damn thing off of him. We finally get it high enough to put it back up on the rack. The weight of the machine had broken two of his ribs. He wasn't a rocket scientist by any means.

BIGGEST MAN IN THE NFL

The key to St. Clair was not only his size but also his strength. At 6' 9', 265 pounds, he would hit that two-man sled so hard that he would not just move it back but literally knock it over!

During one of their practice sessions, coach Red Hickey asked Bob to show the rookie hopefuls at the 49er camp how to hit a tackling dummy. He charged and slammed into the mammoth-dangling dummy they called *Big Bertha*. There was a loud *bang!* Down came Bertha, sawdust and all. It wasn't the chain or the cable that had broken; the dummy itself split apart and broke in two!

49ERS 0 ST. CLAIR 2

We, my wife Ann, my mother and I were coming home from a game at Kezar Stadium. The 49ers had lost. I had been injured the week before and didn't play in this particular game.

We came to a stop sign at 7th and Irving Streets. Many of the fans from the stadium were walking along Irving. Within that group were two guys who obviously had too much to drink. They looked over at the car and said, 'Hey, there's Bob St. Clair. Hey St. Clair, you really blew it. You guys aren't worth a shit!' I got so goddamn mad that I got out of the car. By now they were standing right next to the door. I felt that all I would have to do is stand up and they would get the hell out of there. I stood up, and Bang! - one of the guys hit me from the side. I fell against the car. Then one guy was kind of holding me while I was wrestling with him. That's when a friend of mine was walking by, grabbed one of the guys and pulled him off. By that time I had pushed the first guy away and I whacked him. He went right down. My friend had let the other guy go so I smashed him. The first guy got up. While he was standing there I tackled him head on, lifted him off the ground and running him up on the sidewalk into the side of a building. I put my head right in his stomach and chest. He went right down...out cold. The other guy jumped on top of me and I grabbed him by the hair and smashed him into the sidewalk. The police came by. One of the officers said, 'You had better get out of here. I'll take care of it.' I got back in the car and I was so emotionally involved with what had just happened that the windshields immediately steamed up. I had to put the defroster on to see. I got home and called the Park Station police to see if there was a report. There was, and they told me that both guys had to go to the emergency. The next day there was a big article in the newspaper:

49ERS LOSE BUT ST. CLAIR WINS IN PARKING LOT.

A SUNDAY MORNING RITUAL

One Sunday morning an article about the *ethical character* of the 49ers appeared in the San Francisco Examiner. Our coach, Red Hickey had boasted how this great team of men (even though they haven't won every game) still showed quality and character by attending mass each Sunday before a game. Billy Kilmer tells the real story and how the team eventually converted him to Catholicism.

I had been with the 49ers for two years now. In my first year with the team, nineteen guys would go to Mass on Sunday. Red Hickey was there and they would all go to church. We would have a pre-game meal together.

In my second year I mentioned to Bob about the guys going to Mass on Sunday. He said, 'Why don't you come with us?' I said ok. So we all went to Mass at 7:00 in the morning. There were at least 20 guys there. So we walked into the church and everyone said a prayer; and a couple of times Bob would go into the confessional and I would have to run out of the church because I thought it was going to be struck by lightening and collapse. We weren't in church five minutes when we all turned around and walked out. We went to Bob's manager's house (he managed Bob's liquor stores) where he had set up a whole breakfast table which included three bottles of Old Crow sitting in the middle of the table. We would have coffee

with a couple of shots of Old Crow just before the pre-game meal. We sure

had a good time!

TITTLE HURT – BRODIE GETS THE CALL

In one game in the late 50's, Tittle got hurt and John Brodie, who
was our second string quarterback, was called in to replace him. We were
playing either in Philadelphia or Detroit. John was so nervous. He came
into the huddle, knelt down and looked at all of us. He wanted to say
something but he couldn't talk. When he was finally able to say a word he
began squealing. I looked at him and said, 'What? Say that again.' No
one in the huddle could understand him. He was so nervous. I looked at the
clock and I knew we didn't have time to run a play, so I had to call a time
out. The coach yelled at me. 'Come here St. Clair. What the hell are you
doing calling a time out?' In those days you didn't call a time out unless a
guy died on the field. I told the coach that I realized how precious time outs
were but if he was going to send a quarterback in, he should at least have a
set of balls on him. This guy can't talk! Brodie finally calmed down and
stopped talking like a little girl.

THE SHOTGUN

I guess what a lot of fans remember about the 49ers in those days is the shotgun. I think we all had certain apprehensions about the shotgun offense. Doubts. But we tried it out a few times and all of a sudden it totally befuddled the other team. The first time we used it was against Baltimore in 1960, a very good team. They didn't know what the hell to do. I remember Colts' defensive tackle Artie Donovan and those guys looking around and looking back and forth and saying, 'What the hell is going on here'? By that time we had snapped the ball. We were off and running.

We started using it in 1960. Then at the beginning of '61, Tittle was traded to New York and that was the reason they gave. Tittle didn't fit into that kind of an offense. Tittle was your conventional drop back passer, and a damned good one obviously but not for Red Hickey's idea of revolutionizing football. We had Billy Kilmer, Muddy Waters and Brodie. Those were the shotgun quarterbacks. And Brodie had trouble in that type of position as well. He'd played a T at Stanford. But certainly Billy Kilmer, who in college at UCLA was a tailback, did everything – run, pass, kick – he fit right in. So did Muddy Waters. So this was the wave of the future. It didn't last long.

The explanation of what stopped the shotgun is always given that the Bears moved Bill George over center and crashed him through, but that's oversimplified. See, when you move your guards a yard away from your center, then the tackles two yards out from them the way we did, you have gaping holes. That's the idea, of course. The hole is already there for the runner. But what the Bears did was overload a side with defenders. We had no blockers available to pick up the extra men. And that was it. They would come up with these different stunts where they'd cut two men from guard to center, and Bill George would stunt up the middle. Well, it was like he was on a fast track. No one in between him and the quarterback getting the ball. A field day! And we just weren't able to adjust to that kind of a defense.

We didn't drop the shotgun immediately after that game. We tried to make a few adjustments, but the defenses were on to it. You just couldn't use the shotgun as we did with the split line. They have shotguns today. But it's not the same thing.

Billy Kilmer remembers running the shotgun with Bob was his right tackle.

In my first year as a quarterback with the 49ers, I ran out of the shotgun. You could always rely on Bob. You knew that on that side of the line that no one was going to get to you. You had to keep an eye on the other side of the line, but not on Bob's. I think he was one of the greatest offensive tackles to ever play the game.

Mike McCormick of the Cleveland Browns and Pro Football Hall of Fame member credits Bob with his (McCormick's) reign as captain.

Bob and I played the same position so we were not on the field at the same time. At that time offensive linemen were not very well known. Jerry Kramer of the Green Bay Packers used to say, 'If you want to commit a murder and hide out, become a lineman in the NFL and no one will ever find you.'

I credit Bob with my being captain of the Browns so long. One year we were out in San Francisco playing an exhibition game against the 49ers. Our captains were a defensive back and a receiver. The San Francisco captains were Bob St. Clair and Leo Nomellini. I happened to be standing next to our coach, Paul Brown. He looked over at me and said, 'Hell, they have us outsized already'!

So the next week Don Colo, a defensive lineman, and myself were named the permanent team captains of the Browns.

Offensive linemen usually watch other offensive linemen in game films. I used to watch Bob and how he played the defense of other teams. He was so tall and his legs were so long that it was a natural asset to the three-point stance position.

I tried to mimic Bob's position, but my legs weren't as long as his. I was almost out of the NFL permanently because I couldn't adapt to his way of playing.

He's a great person and a heck of a guy.

THE HEAD SLAP AND THE LEG WHIP:
ST. CLAIR'S RECOLLECTION

One of the best defensive ends in the league who made the head slap part of his repertoire before it was legal was Deacon Jones. I would take a pair of shin guards and put them on the back of my legs (on my calves) and put my socks over the guards so you couldn't see it. I would use this when I would cross body block and leg whip. I can remember so well that a couple of times Deacon thought he was by me and then he would make the mistake to move to the outside. That's when I would do a cross body block on him. He would reverse his direction, come back and step over my calf. That's when I would hit him somewhere in the chest or stomach – knocking him out flat and knocking the wind out of him.

THE HEAD SLAP AND THE LEG WHIP:
JONES' RECOLLECTION

That legwhip was just his lousy blocking technique.

The guy was 6'9' and all legs. He would kick that leg up when you would beat him. If you beat him and you were coming up around the corner up come the leg...with him being so tall. I was a

rookie and I couldn't get out of the way of the damned thing. I really

didn't understand what he was doing to me. He would kick me and

trip me. Do all kinds of funky things to me. He was a veteran and he

really abused me my first and second year. He was a bonafide all-

pro at that point. He used all these tricks that I had never known

anyone to do. I'm 6'5' and he would kick me in the chest!

I didn't headslap on Bob too much because I hadn't yet

mastered the move. I just wish I could have played against him later

on in my career when I knew what the hell I was doing!

He was a hell of an athlete and played with some great

football players like Ollie Matson and Gino Marchetti. I played

against both Matson and Marchetti and have great respect for them.

They were the real pioneers of the game. Football was different in

those days. You had to really love it to play it. It wasn't about the

money. You could make more money doing something else. It was

about eleven guys getting' together and havin' fun. Today's players

don't have fun. They make big money but it's like a chore for them

to go to work. The players in my time and Bob's time loved going to

work.

Tommy Wilson of the Los Angeles Rams tells about an overly confident rookie, Deacon Jones who told the press that he was going to 'eat up St. Clair' during their first gridiron meeting.

Deacon was a rookie with the Rams in 1959 or 1960, and he was cut from the team after the last exhibition game, which was played on a Saturday night. The following day I was getting ready to take Deacon to the airport. He was returning home. Before I left, I received a call from the Rams that Gene Brito, the Rams' defensive end who was taken from the Washington Redskins, had died, and to not take Deacon to the airport. He had just made the team because of Brito's passing. This was very rare.

Deacon was now playing first string. He had a lot of mouth. He was very fast. In the fourth game of the season we were on our way to San Francisco to play the 49ers. The 49ers had a great 6'9' OT named Bob St. Clair who just beats up on DE's.

Deacon took it to the press and told them that he understands that Bob St. Clair eats red, raw meat. Deacon then tells them that he is going to eat some raw meat this Sunday because he is going to eat up Bob St. Clair. And this was in the newspaper.

We played the game on Sunday and won. The next day we went to practice to watch the game films. As we were watching, the defensive line coach Don Paul yells, 'Turn off that damn camera! Where's Deacon

Jones? Stand up! The next time you're gonna tell the press you're going to eat somebody up, hell, you haven't crossed the line of scrimmage ALL DAY! Instead of Bob St. Clair eating raw meat he ate Black meat. He ate your Black butt up Sunday. And next time you ever want to tell the press what you're going to do, you better back it up!' Deacon said in a humble, sobering voice, ' I will get him the next time, coach.'

WHO MISSED THE LINEBACKER?

It was 1954 and we were playing the Chicago Bears. In those days the goal posts were right on the goal line and were all padded. We were coming down the field for a td and were on the 1-yard line. The post was on my left and the guard's right. It was almost like they had another man on the line. We had just called a play where our fullback, Joe Perry was to take a direct handoff into the line. He took the hand off and ran directly smack dab into the goal post with his head, veered a little to the right and went across the goal line and scored. I helped him get up and back to the huddle. He was dizzy and his eyes were going back and forth. Just before we lined up for the conversion he said, 'Bob that was a mighty fine hole you opened up for me, but tell me one thing; which one of you bastards missed that linebacker?'

BLOCKING FOR MAC AND WOODSON

Hugh McElhenny was 6'1' and weighed 205. He was tough, casual, impulsive, and short tempered – and viewed both football and life 'as fun'. He was nicknamed 'The King' and will remain an icon of pro football's fabulous fifties. In a practical sense, he left his mark on the era. He was the first of the 'specialty' running backs to rest when the other team had the ball and concentrate on doing what he did best. He also didn't play defense. He helped start the 'age of the specialist'.

In 1961 Red Hickey, then coach of the 49ers (whom he did not get along) released him into the expansion draft by sending him to the Minnesota Vikings. Hickey had the option to trade him – but chose to let the future Hall of Fame member go for nothing in return.

When we played, we had so much pride in our personal performance as it affected the team. We would play as a unit. I used to get great pleasure of leading McElhenny around the end and seeing the cornerback come up. I would smile because nine out of ten times I knew I would nail that sucker because of my range.

The most successful play that Mac and I ran together was the 'quick toss' around the right side. Mac was the right halfback and I was the right tackle and I would pull. The end would block down and then we would have a flanker on the right who would block down and get that defensive end. I would pull around the back of the defensive end. Once I cleared him I would just flatten the defensive halfback and Mac would just scream one way or the other. As soon as I would hit a guy I would immediately jump up because I knew somewhere during that run that I would get another block. Mac's running style caused him to be all over the field. He would first go completely over to the left side and then swing back to the other side. As he was coming back across the field I would get a blindside. I loved those kinds of situations. You would see this guy getting ready to tackle and you would clear him out and knock his helmet off.

In a memorable performance against the Los Angeles Rams in 1959, St. Clair convoyed teammate Abe Woodson on Woodson's 105-yard kickoff return. Game films showed that fourteen blocks helped clear the way for Woodson with Bob contributing to six of them. Out of those six, two Rams were put 'out of commission' for the remainder of the game.

I always played on the right side and on run backs I would call left, right or middle. This particular time I played on the right side in which I would go across to where the wall of blockers was coming down when they kicked off. When Abe Woodson got the ball in the end zone, I came across and hit my guy into another guy. I immediately got up and started going to the right side and saw Abe running through the pile. This allowed me to get a blindside that knocked out two or three guys. As soon as I got up Abe was coming back across the field. I was able to get in another block or so. I ended up blocking six Rams.

The fans will always jump up and carry a guy on their shoulders because he's run 40 yards. Meanwhile nobody comes out to help the three or four linemen out of the mud who knocked themselves out to spring the back loose.

A SOBERING LESSON

In his rookie season with the New York Giants, Sam Huff was standing idly by a pileup when St. Clair spotted him. To this day, Bob still laughs when talking about 'popping' Huff. Like most lineman St. Clair got a big kick out of belting a defensive player, especially one as good as Huff.

There was nothing really personal about this type of contact. Most linemen of the 50's considered it their job to hurt each other and that they did - but only in the friendliest of ways.

St. Clair's joy out of belting another man senseless stemmed simply from the fact that he could not win recognition by any other means. He was an offensive lineman, in an era where the cheers were for the quarterbacks, halfbacks, ends, and the defense. Nobody loved, or for that matter, cared about the five men over the ball, from tackle to tackle.

Standing by a pileup is a typical rookie trick. You learn that in college. You know, never pile on, and all the rest of the Queensbury twaddle. So you stop short, say, 'Oops, sorry,' and there you are, all off balance, a fat target.

I saw Sam Huff standing like that. Man, you can hit them so hard when they're off balance; they'll think their head was on a swivel. You can really pick 'em off that way.

Huff's recollection is not much different than that of St. Clair's.

Bob blindsided me and cut me in half. It was a sobering lesson for me. I no longer stood by while players piled on. I jumped on, like the rest.

DEAD OF WINTER AND NO FACILITIES

We had a game in Green Bay – but the stadium had no facilities at that time. We had to change after breakfast at the hotel and leave with our uniforms on (tape and all) and get on the bus.

At half time we went up in the stands on one side of the field and they went on the other. There were no dressing rooms. We had some barrels filled with burning wood. We were huddled around the barrels shivering. The coaches were describing the offensive and defensive plays, but no one was listening. It was so damn cold. After the ball game, we had to get back on the bus and go downtown to the hotel. When we arrived we had to walk through the hotel – our cleats covered in mud and snow, tape unraveling off our hands and legs. We were a mess.

CAPTAIN'S REVENGE

Gordy Soltau, former 49er kicker refers fondly to Bob as 'Our Policeman'.

He was our policeman. When someone on the other team would take a cheap shot at one of us, 2-3 plays later they would meet up with Bob. He would seek them out. He was very good at downfield blocking. They would usually end up on the deck!

88

R. C. Owens, otherwise known as the 'Alley Oop' – a tremendous end for the 49ers in the 50's says that Bob was the 'total package'.

Bob was the total package: big, strong, fast, tough and mean. I don't think I could explain him any better. As a friend, he is always there for you. He's there when you need him most, when you are up or down....a guy that you would say, 'I just love this guy.' A guy you would do anything for. If you needed advice, he was the guy to give it. You trusted his suggestion. He was a great leader. He was a Frank Buck kind of guy....a Frank Buck kind of leader.

Bob used to like to leave his mark. And when he left his mark you always knew it. Because in combat he always dominated his opponent and in the end he would stand over him like Goliath saying you SOB. You knew that he was on your side, and that he was really great individual. I used to always s like to see him in battle. If there was an argument between the opponent and a player from our team, he always seemed to be in the arena. He was always the big protector. He was always there in your defense.

Bob wouldn't tolerate racism. He proved this to fullback J. D. Smith in a game against the Colts.

We were playing the Colts in Baltimore. I played the fullback position. On this particular play, I ran through the line and popped this big tackle. Boom...he went right up and then down. He said, 'You goddamned nigger!' All at once, Bob grabbed him by the neck. I had to pull Bob off of him. Right then I knew that Bob was my man for the next hundred years

Back in the 50's when we were playing the Chicago Bears, at Kezar Stadium....we were in the middle of the game and I led Mac around the end and threw a block and got up immediately and chased him and he went by and he finally got tackled right in front of the Chicago Bear bench. And as he went down, just before the half...he was trying to get up real fast because time was running out. He was trying to get up and the guys on top were holding him down. So he kicked the guy to get the hell off of him. And when he did that, he stood up...I was running full speed right at him and I saw this guy with an overcoat on with a hat and glasses running out from the Bear bench on to the field. As Mac was running back to the huddle, the guy in the overcoat kicked him right in the ass. And as he did that, Mac went sprawling forward. This guy turned around just as I was going by him and I whacked him on the side of the neck with an elbow as I ran by him knocking his hat and glasses off and him down. As I stopped and turned around, all the Bears ran off their bench and jumped on top of me. We were fighting and it was a hell of a mess. And I found out later, after the ball game was over, that I had whacked George Halas, the Bears' coach.

The interesting thing about that...in those days nobody got penalized for that stuff....but right after the season was over George Halas called up Tony Moribito (Tony told me this) and said that he wanted to trade for me. 'Any guy who has that spirit and is a good athlete I want him!' said Halas. But Tony said no way and he didn't trade me. But I was probably one of the very few guys that ever hit Halas when he was an older guy.

THE GAME OF THEIR LIVES

Sportswriter, Bob Carroll talks about the 1957 playoff game between San Francisco and Detroit.

It wasn't until late in the decade, of course, that pro football came to be thought of as a part of the American culture. If you could freeze any one moment in 49er history and say this is when it happened, you probably would be looking at the 1957 playoff game, and Detroit's remarkable comeback win over San Francisco – certainly the most important game ever played at that time by the Forty Niners.

We had a playoff game with Detroit to see who would be the Western Division champs and who would go to the Championship Game (which is now known as the Super Bowl) to play Cleveland. The Browns were the champions of their division. We had played Cleveland in an exhibition game and beat them badly. Now, all we had to do is get over Detroit. We had split with the Lions during the year. We were very confident about winning. We came out of Kezar Stadium smokin'! Bobby Layne was the Lions' starting quarterback. During the first half we jumped out to a big lead. We were 24-7 at halftime.

As we ran off the field we could hear the champagne corks going off. The fans were celebrating already.

Talk about being overconfident! Jim David, Lions' defensive back later told me this.

'The walls were paper thin between the locker rooms at Kezar. The 49ers were really celebrating. We could hear, 'Where are you going to spend your money?' 'I'm gong to get a new car.' You could hear all this stuff going on from the 49er locker room during the half.'

In the Lions' locker room Joe Schmidt, linebacker was rallying the troops,

'The public address announcer was announcing that anybody interested in obtaining championship tickets they would be on sale the following week. I told the guys that they are already

selling championship tickets…that's exactly how they (the 49ers) feel

about you (the Lions). Let's go out and play a tough second half and

see what can happen.'

All of a sudden during the 3rd quarter they put in quarterback

Tobin Rote. Our defensive backs all seemed to get hurt during the

beginning of that 3rd quarter. All three backs went down. Poor

Frankie Albert, our coach, was looking up and down the row to see

whom we could put in. We had only 33 players but we didn't have

anymore defensive backs. We had offensive backs but they didn't

know how to play defense – so what happened was that Tobin had a

field day taking advantage of inexperienced guys who didn't know

the defensive back position.

We took the opening kickoff and Mac had a long run on the

first play. We were down on the 4 or 5-yard line – first and goal.

We ran two plays and it was now third down. Perry took a direct

hand off over me on the line and scored; but the referee had thrown a

flag and said that I was off sides. It moved us back 5 yards. Now,

Tittle tried to pass and it was incomplete. We had to kick a field

goal. If we had scored that td, it would have been enough that

Detroit could not have made it back. It was now 27-7 and they began

going up and down the field. They killed us.

The following day we were watching the game films and it showed that I wasn't off sides but I was ahead of everyone else. I had such a quick start when the ball was snapped, that I was way ahead of everyone. I had moved the same time that the ball was snapped. If the referee had seen what really had happened, I'm sure we would have won. We were confident as hell at halftime. We were really ready to go. That was shown when Mac ran the ball all the way down the field. We should have scored. As for many of the players on that '57 team, it still hurts to talk about it to this day.

This next section could be titled 'Gridiron Follies'. You'll realize why as you read along. Just remember, it's the 50's. Football didn't have all the rules and regulations that it has today. Thank God!

THE HULA BOWL

In 1957 I broke my shoulder in the beginning of the season and I wasn't expected to play. I, instead, made a miraculous recovery and was able to come back. I had missed 7 games and ended up missing the Pro Bowl because they pick the players early in the season. Instead, I was invited to play in the Hula Bowl. In those days, in 1957, the Hula Bowl was made up of just a handful of pros and the other part of the team was made up of the servicemen from Pearl Harbor, Hickem Field etc. They were the servicemen All Stars. They had their best players with us and we would play the College All Americans.

I can remember when we were all practicing on this big open field. The college team was on one end of the field and we were on the other. They were all in full pads and everything else...they were hot and ready to go. We had our shorts on with leis around our necks. It was warm and we were running just a few basic plays and patterns and so forth. Then we would run across the field to the liquor store across the street and buy a bunch of beer.

We came back, sat in the shade and watched these guys practice. They were scrimmaging. We were drinking beer and clapping when someone would make a good play. I can remember Charlie Kruger who was playing on the All American team said to me many years later that when we were out there practicing and we looked at all you guys, we said, 'We're going to kill these old guys. Look at them. They are so out of shape, drinking and smoking.'

Well, it was the beginning of the game – the first play. They kicked off. The ball lands in the end zone and we take it from the 20. On the first play Crazy Legs Hirsch went 80 yards for a TD. We kicked off to them. They couldn't score. Every time we got the ball we scored. Tobin Rote to Frank Gifford....Tobin Rote to Hirsch and on and on. Finally we got the word from the other bench to stop passing and make the game more interesting. It was the first quarter and the score was 28-0. They asked us to try and keep the ball on the ground. So instead of passing we threw a couple of little dink passes, swing outs and so forth.

The next play was to have Joe Perry take a hand-off up the middle. We had a trap play and Joe took the ball from the 35 yard line....Bingo! He breaks through for a TD. Now its 35-0 – still the first quarter. We were killing them.

In the second half Frank Gifford had taken a pitch out from Rote. Frank cut back and was tackled. There was a pile up. I was running full speed towards the pile when I noticed Alex Karras coming the other way. Instead of throwing his body on the pile he was trying to dance around it. He was off balance when I hit him full speed right in the chest with my helmet knocking his helmet off and turning him upside down. I looked down at him and said, 'Welcome to the NFL kid.' And I helped him up. He told me later, 'You know that was the hardest hit I had ever taken.' He learned a lesson that you don't tip toe around a pile.

When I returned from the Hula Bowl I told the 49er coach, 'You know, coach, you might have made a mistake in drafting this kid, Charlie Krueger. He's a big skinny kid (around 230 lbs) and all that but unless he puts on weight he will never make the team!' Krueger later went on to make All Pro (three times) with the 49ers. Shows you how much I knew.

WIPEOUT AT WAIKIKI

New York Giants halfback and Hall of Fame member, Frank Gifford recalls teaching St. Clair how to waterski at Waikiki.

Bob and I played together in the 1957 Hula Bowl. It was at that time that I took Bob out on the ocean for his first waterskiing lesson. He had never skied before. I got in the water with him and showed him how to get up. 'Just hold on' I said. But each time he tried to stand up he would end up swallowing water because it was hitting him in the face. Down he would go. Finally he got up half way. When Bob said, 'Hit it' I took off with the boat. He was fighting the water, trying to keep his knees bent and holding on to the rope when, 'Bang', the rope broke. He had pulled on the rope so hard that he tore the bolts (which held the rope) right out from the back of the boat!

I came around to pick him up. He wanted to try it again. I told him, 'You broke the boat. I don't think waterskiing is your kind of sport, Bob.

SOAP BOX DERBY

Since the beginning of professional football, football players have always known how to have a good time, but their efforts often ended like some kind of Daffy Duck cartoon.

One year we were playing an exhibition game in Akron, Ohio. The stadium where we were practicing was also used for the Soap Box Derby Nationals. They had a long hill behind the stadium complete with hey bales and all. I talked one of our quarterbacks, Hal Ledger, into taking one of the soap boxes up the hill. I couldn't sit in it so he sat inside and I straddled the back and held on to him. All the guys were at the bottom of the hill cheering us on. Well, we started going down the hill and we were really going fast. I still had my sweats and cleats on because we had just finished practice. I put my cleats on the track to slow us down and it burned my cleats off. It didn't slow us down a bit. We finally ran into the hay bale at the bottom of the hill. I went flying out and skidding on to the track. Hal didn't get hurt at all, but I had all these burns up my leg and my ass. I didn't want to tell the coach. I had to play two days later. The trainer saw what had happened and said, 'Jesus Christ! What happened to you?' 'Never mind, never mind', I said. He bandaged me up so well that the only time it hurt was the initial skid on the field. But after the game the entire inside of my pant leg was covered in blood. The coach never found out.

THE TRIP PLAY

One year in the late '50's, we were having a bad season. We were standing in that dusty west tunnel waiting to go onto the field before a game and the fans already were booing like hell. Y.A. Tittle, who was going to be introduced first, said, 'Bob please, you go first.'

I was the team captain so I agreed. When I ran out, I forgot there was this little border about 5 inches high on the track. The fans were booing so loudly I turned to hear them, missed the step and went sprawling. The people were laughing and clapping. At least they stopped booing. I was now on the sidelines standing next to Dan Colchico and the band was playing the national anthem. Dan turned to me and said, 'Good job, Robert! Are you ready or are you ready!

MOSES COMES TO THE MOUNTAIN

I had missed six weeks of games after my shoulder surgery. The 49ers were at Bear Mountain, New York, preparing to play the Giants. They had lost three in a row and were badly dispirited when the door to the lobby of the Bear Mountain Inn suddenly flung open, and I strode into the room and announced: 'I am Moses. I come to lead the 49ers out of the wilderness'.

The following Sunday, with snow on the ground, we upset the Giants, 27-17. We closed out the season with wins over the Colts and the Packers, for an 8-4 record.

'HEY ST. CLAIR! IT'S HAPPY HOUR!'

One year, Vince Lombardi, the famous Packers' coach, was named as coach of the Pro Bowl. In those days they had the Pro Bowl in Los Angeles. I remember this one year when Doug Atkins (who was my height and my size) and I had gone. We had been to quite a few Pro Bowls before. Each year we would report to the hotel and sit in a room where the coach went over procedure, times of practice and so on, and then would tell you he'd see you tomorrow. Well, Vince Lombardi was so gung ho that he started the meeting off with a Knute Rockne speech. I was sitting in the front of the room and Doug was sitting in the back.

Lombardi went on and on about practice and then he began writing plays and x's and o's on the blackboard. We're all looking at our watches thinking we want to get out of here. We had our keys in our hands and wanted to go back to our rooms and unpack. Anyway...Lombardi continued writing offensive patterns and so on on the board. All of a sudden from the back of the room I heard Doug Atkins say in a real loud voice, 'Hey St. Clair! Ca'mon. We gotta go across the street. It's happy hour at the Brown Derby. (The Brown Derby was across the street from where we were staying at the Ambassador Hotel.) Ask him what time the bus leaves and let's get the hell out of here.'

Lombardi turned around and everyone was dead silent...except Doug who's still talking. 'Come on St. Clair. God damn it, come on!' I'm shrinking down in the chair putting my hand over my head thinking, 'Oh shit'. Lombardi put the chalk down and said, 'You're right, Doug. I'm gonna let you guys go so you can relax. Tomorrow we have practice and tomorrow we'll start getting serious about this game. Thanks for coming, fellas. We'll see you at 9:00 tomorrow.' I thought I was going to die! Doug was nuttier than a fruitcake. He used to tell me that when he was practicing at Wrigley Field he used to bring a .22 out there to shoot the pigeons in the rafters. Used to drive Halas crazy!

CHICAGO MAFIA

In 1956 Lou Palatella, the 49er guard, and I were in Chicago. Lou told me he had met this guy in Miami who gave him his card. The guy told him to look him up if he was ever in Chicago. Lou asked me, 'Do you want to go out to dinner with him?' The guy's name was Guigo. He was an Italian who lived on the West side. So we took a cab over to see him. He had a liquor and grocery store. To get there we had to go through the stockyards. I'm looking at Lou thinking, 'What the hell did you get me into. '

We stopped in front of the store and it looked like one of those Mom and Pop stores in San Francisco. We walked in and Lou told the clerk, 'My name is Lou Palatella and I came to see Guigo. I called him and he told me to be here. ' The guy said, 'Just a minute.' Then another guy came over and the clerk talked to him. Pretty soon this little dapper guy walks out and says, 'Follow me.' That wasn't Guigo...it was someone else. We walked to the end of one of the aisles of the store...there were no doors...I wondered where the hell we were going. All of a sudden one of the panels (where the groceries were) opened up. We walked through it to an ally way. The panel closed behind us. We walked into this room. There was this guy in there wearing a sleeveless white t-shirt with the shoulder holster and gun. Guigo came in and Lou hugged him. Guigo said, 'We go eat, we go eat.'

I went to leave by the street door and one of the guys grabbed me and pushed me back holding his hand to my chest. This guy stayed by the door and another guy walked out to the street to the limo. He opened the door and stood between the door and the limo. Then the other guy who was standing at the door escorted me to the limo and then returned to escort Lou. Guigo is surrounded by three guys as he is being escorted to the car.

When we got to the restaurant, same thing - we couldn't get out till they said we could. But before we got out of the car I saw a group of people leaving the restaurant. They were very angry. What had happened was that Guigo's gang members went in and told everyone that they had to *get the hell out!* His boys paid for all of their dinners, but they had to leave....now. Each of us was again escorted into the restaurant. Once we got inside, they locked the door. One of the guys stood by the door the entire time; another stood behind us the entire time. We ate and talked. I said to Lou on the way back, 'That was one hell of an experience! Where in the hell do you meet these people?'

DETROIT MAFIA

One evening after the Detroit game, we were down at *The Red Rooster*. It was a bar and restaurant on the river. We were drinking pretty heavily. Well, you know, after a game you are pretty dehydrated and you have to drink lots of fluids. All of a sudden I heard a *whack*. It was someone getting hit by a fist. I turned around and looked and I saw some of the people picking up our assistant coach. I went over to him and said, 'Geez, Coach...what happened?' He said, 'That guy over there copped a Sunday on me.' I said, 'What guy?' I walked over to the bar and said, 'This guy?' He said, 'No'. 'This guy?' He said, 'No'. 'This one?' He said, 'Yeah.' And I tapped the guy and the guy wouldn't turn around. I tapped him again. He was still ignoring me. So I kind of grabbed him by the shoulder and turned him around on the stool. And I said, 'Hey listen, I'm talking to you. He said, 'You don't want any trouble with me.' 'I want to ask you why you hit my friend over here?' He said, 'I told you - you don't want any trouble with me. You can't win this fight.' I said, 'What! You little pipsqueak!' And I reached around and grabbed him by the lapels of his jacket and swung him around. As I went to lift him I felt a very strong object in my pelvis and as I looked down between my arms and there was a gun...a .38 special. So I released his jacket automatically. And I said, 'I see your point that I'm not going to win this. We won't bother you any more sir.' I turned around and Leo (Nomellini) said, 'Take him outside, Bob. Take him outside!' I said, 'Leo, we are leaving! Tell the guys we're out of here!' So we all left and they all said, 'What's the matter, are you crazy? Go get that guy and bring him out here.' I said, 'I'll talk to you outside, I'll talk to you outside!' When we got outside I told them that he had a gun on me. We can't fool with him. We don't know how many other guys in there are his friends! They all might be packin'! We were out of there!

MILWAUKEE MAFIA

The 49ers were in Milwaukee to play the Packers at Milwaukee Municipal Stadium. One evening we were all sitting around having a drink at the bar.

A few minutes later several women came in. They sat near us. One of the women there was named Angelina. In a minute, I'll tell you why I remember her name so distinctly.

Anyway, we struck up a conversation and I mentioned to her that I was with the 49ers. She told me that she was with the wedding party that was in the room next door to the bar. She said that she would have liked for me to have joined her at the reception, but she knew that *the family* would not agree to *an outsider*. She finished her drink, said good-bye and returned to the party.

The next day, which was the day before the game, Tittle and I were in our room when we heard a knock on the door. Tittle answered the door. Outside were two big guys standing there in dark suits, dark shirts and white ties. They had asked to see me.

Tittle came running back into the room. 'Jesus Christ! What did you do now?' he said. 'What are you talkin' about?' I said. Y was really nervous. 'There are two guys, big guys, at the door who want to see you. They don't look very good.'

I went to the door. One of the guys said (in a heavy Italian accent), 'Bob St. a Clair? I have a message for a you from a the ___ family. You are a nice a young a man and you have a long career in the football. The family does a not want to a see anything happen to a you.' What I didn't know was that Tittle was in the other room listening to all of this. 'The family would a like for a you to not see Angelina.'

'First of all, who is Angelina?' I said. 'She was the woman you were a talking to a yesterday at a the bar.' I explained the situation to him. 'She came out to the bar (from the reception) with a group of women. They sat down with us. All we did was have a drink and talk a little. Then she returned to the reception. That was it. Nothing else happened. Why are you telling me this?'

'You don't a quite understand. You want to continue to play the football?' he said. I saw that this conversation was going nowhere. Finally I said, 'I think I get the message.' With that, the two men left.

I closed the door and Tittle said, 'Are you crazy? You're going to get us killed!' 'Will you stop it, Y! I said.

The next day was the game. We were standing under the bleachers in the stadium waiting to go out and be introduced. I was the captain then. Tittle was the quarterback and usually went first. Next was Brodie and then I went behind him.

All of a sudden Tittle ran up to the guy who announced the players. Panicking, he said, 'He's the captain of the team (pointing to me). He goes first.' I looked at Y and said, 'What the hell's wrong with you?' 'They are going to kill somebody, he said. They want you, not me. I don't even want to be close to you. You go out first!' He thought for sure they had the cross hairs on me as I ran out on to the field.

PLAYING WITH PAIN - THE HOOKED TESTICLE

When we were at the St. Mary's college campus during the pre season, Ed Henke (49er defensive end) and I would always go deer hunting together.

One night Ed and I were out (after a team meeting). We spotted this deer near a barbed wire fence and whacked him with a .38. The deer went down. We went running over to pick it up and the deer got up and jumped over the fence. Ed said, 'I'll go this way and you go that way'. I climbed over the barbed wire fence and was running along one side of the hill and he was running along the other.

All of a sudden while I was running I stopped. The ground started shaking and I heard this noise. What had happened is that Ed had scared this herd of cows. They were running right at me. It was dark and I couldn't see them, so I took off running back to where I was. By this time Ed had come back and swung around. He didn't see the deer either so he came back and followed me. Now we were both standing there while this herd of cows was coming straight at us. I jumped over the fence and cleared it. He jumped over just as the cows ran into the fence.

We finally went back with a flashlight, found the deer and put it in the car. When we got back into the car Ed took the flashlight and pointed it to his groin. There was blood all over the place! I said, 'Oh, my God! Jesus Christ, you must have really cut yourself!'

We went back to the dressing room and Ed sat on the training table. Ted Connolly came in and said, 'What the hell is going on'? By that time Ed had taken off his pants. He had ripped his Levis trying to clear the barbed wire fence and in doing so, ripped open the sac on his testicle. His testicle was hanging through. He needed to have it stitched. I said, 'Go get the doctor'.

This was on a Wednesday night and the regular doctor was off on Wednesday night so we had to call on the other doctor who was retired and there only part time. He had been down at the bar all night. He had half a heat on. We finally got him out of bed...he was shaking but we eventually got him over to the training facility.

The doctor put the light on Ed. He said, 'We'll have to stitch that.' I asked if he was going to give him Novocain. 'I don't have Novocain'. he said. Just then I remembered something that I had seen in the movies. I took a towel, wet it and wrapped it in a circle. I told Ed to hold it in his mouth, like biting the bullet.

Next, Leo (Nomellini) took one leg and I took the other. Ted held the light and held up the sac of his testicle so that the doctor could stitch it up. The needle was actually a hook.

The doctor made the first stitch and Ed bit down hard on the towel. Everything was gong real smooth until the fourth stitch. As the doctor began to make the stitch he leaned over Ed as though he was going to pass out. When he tried to pull the stitch through, he went right through the testicle with the hook and through the outside of the sac. Ed came right off the table screaming and yelling. We put the towel back in his mouth. The doctor finally finished.

The following day we had practice. I asked Ed how he was. He said he was fine. When we got into the showers after practice I asked Ed how the stitches were. I could see that one testicle was fine but the other had a tuck in it from where the stitch had caught both the testicle and the sac. We nicknamed him *One Hung Low*.

A FOOT IN THE MOUTH

Former Los Angeles Ram and Hall of Fame member, Tom Fears said this about tackling in his era.

Your face took one tremendous beating when you would tackle and hit people. That's the way you were taught. If you didn't lose any teeth or didn't have a broken nose you were considered a pansy of a player'

Although my regular position was OT, my height made me a natural when opponents lined up to kick. Of the ten kicks I blocked in the 1956 season, there's one that I will never forget.

We were playing the Los Angeles Rams in Los Angeles. Leo Nomellini told me that he noticed that Van Brocklin took three steps when he kicked the ball. He told me to line up over the center and he would line up to his left. When they snapped the ball, he would grab the guard and bring him right through the center and for me to just follow him.

Fourth down and here we go. They snap the ball. Leo picked up the guard and smashed through the center. I leaned back and had a clear shot at the kicker. I was in there so quickly that instead of blocking the ball right after Van Brocklin punted it, I knocked the ball away from the kicker's foot and got kicked square in the teeth. I lost five teeth in that one play.

Now I'm on the ground looking for my teeth. Aware of my condition, the referee called time out. Obviously dazed, I left for the sidelines where the trainer shoved cotton into the orifices which once held my teeth. Without missing a down, I went back into the game and on the next play blocked my opponent allowing the running back to score.

About a quarter later into the game Leo came back and said. 'Hey Bob, I think we can do it this time! ' I told him to 'Get the hell out of here!'

The following week we played the Giants. Defensive back Emlen Tunnell intercepted a Tittle pass on his own 20 and headed up field. Tunnell had outrun all defenders by midfield and was on the 49er 30 when he looked behind him. I was bearing down on him. I caught Tunnell and brought him down on the 20. That was the biggest, personal thrill of my professional career not to mention that I still didn't have my teeth!

THE ROGUE PATIENT

I had just had an operation. The guys used to sneak a ton of liquor into my room. The nurses would constantly tell me that *these people and their liquor* could no longer visit with me in the room.

The next morning they brought me my breakfast along with some apple juice. Again, some of my friends were there with me. A nurse came into the room and told everyone that they had to leave. I told her that they were not leaving and for her to get out. I then got the idea to take the apple juice and pour it in the urine holder. Later the nurse came back into the room and said, 'You're urine looks a little cloudy today, Mr. St. Clair.' So I said, 'Here let me run it through again.' And drank it. Gasping, the nurse went running out of the room.

OTHERWISE, I'M PRETTY LUCKY

As a 49ers rookie in 1953, I broke my back in the Bears game. I had two bones broken in the transverse process in the lower back in three places. They usually put you in traction for that. Instead I wore a plastic jacket and played the next game against Pittsburgh. Remember, if we didn't play, we didn't get paid!

In 1957, I broke my shoulder in a game and went on and played eight more minutes before going to the sidelines.

I was knocked out of action in 1957 for seven games with a shoulder separation that required surgery. I didn't leave the game until eight minutes after I was injured!

In 1962 I missed a few games when I tore an Achilles' tendon. As everyone knows, that's a career ender. Luckily I was back as a regular tackle in 1963 and won the Len Eshmont Award as Most Inspirational 49er.

A second Achilles' injury finally ended my career in 1964.

Even with the numerous concussions, broken bones and loss of teeth, I consider myself to be 'pretty lucky'.

HEY, GOT A SMOKE?

Like I mentioned before, you didn't waste a time out unless a player died on the field. In today's game, players leave the field for something as minor as a jammed finger or turf toe. Turf toe, what a joke! Anyway, that's the way things were in the 50's. A good friend and college teammate of mine and member of the Detroit Lions championship teams of the 50's is guard Dick Stanfel. This is what happened to him when he got hurt on a cold, winter's day playing in Green Bay against the Packers in 1954.

I was playing for Detroit back in 1954 and we were playing in Green

Bay. They didn't have Lambeau Field yet, so we played at a high school

stadium. The fans were right behind us and the bench was against a concrete

wall. I will never forget….I got hurt – it felt like a hip pointer. We couldn't

take a time out because Bobby Layne wouldn't let us take a time out. He

wanted to save all his time outs for the final 2-minute drill. It was finally the

half and I went into the dressing room to be examined. The doctor also thought

it was a hip pointer, so they decided to give me a shot of Novocain. They shot

me once and I told them it didn't take. They shot me again, and I told them it

still didn't take. They shot me a third time and I said, 'Just forget about it – I'll

play without it.'

The following day I couldn't get out of bed. Joe Schmidt was my

roommate. He had to help me get out of bed. He brought me down to the

doctor. The doctor x-rayed my back and told me that I had three broken

bones in my back. They put a corset on me and in a couple of weeks I

played. I had trouble playing because I couldn't get into a three-point

stance.

I started the second half but couldn't play much. I got hit and they

had to take me out. I was on the bench and it was a cold day. The

opponent's bench was right up against the wall of the stadium. You could

literally reach up and touch the fans.

114

I had my hood over me and boy, was I hurtin'. I turned around to one of the fans at Green Bay (he had a Detroit hat on so I knew he was one of ours) and said, 'Hey buddy, you got a cigarette.' He said, 'Yeah.' I said, 'Give me one will you please?' He lit it and gave it to me. That was one of the things that we did in those days....have a cigarette on the bench.

A CLASSY GROUP OF GUYS

I played with and against some of the greatest players ever to play the game. One of those players (as I had previously mentioned) was Dick Stanfel, who played with the Detroit Lions and Washington Redskins. I consider him one of the best blocking guards the league has ever seen.

And what a line up we had at USF in 1951! Ten of the starting eleven were drafted by the pros and three of us made it to the Pro Football Hall of Fame: Ollie Matson (Los Angeles Rams, halfback); Gino Marchetti (Baltimore Colts, defensive end) and me (San Francisco 49ers, offensive tackle). I consider each guy on that squad a class act.

The 49ers had some terrific players too. Jimmy Johnson was one of the best defensive backs in the history of the game. He played about fifteen years, and you could ask anybody who played against him and they'll say he covered them like a glove. Teams would stay away from his area. In a crucial time of the game they would *never* throw in his area. Great ability to cover and he was a hitter too!

John Brodie was better than any other passer we had during my time with the 49ers. But he wasn't built like Y.A. Tittle or Billy Kilmer. He was a true, stay-in-the-pocket, throw-strikes type of quarterback. He wasn't a scrambler who wanted to get out in the heavy traffic and often ran out of bounds. That wasn't what his job was supposed to be, and he took a great deal of criticism for covering up and taking sacks rather than throw the ball and get totally wiped out. Physically he wasn't that kind of a player. But he had a great record and a helluva career.

I wouldn't trade the guys I played with and against for any other era in pro football. They were the best!

GINO MARCHETTI – MY NEMESIS

Gino Marchetti was in a class of his own. It's no wonder he was voted Defensive Player of the Millennium in 2000.

If Marchetti got his hands on me in that first burst, he could control me. So I had to give ground slowly, chop at him and hold him off as long as I could. Gino brought out the best in me, just as I brought out the best in him.

49ers quarterback Billy Kilmer said this about the battles between Gino and me.

Marchetti was one of the finest defensive ends in pro football. He was St. Clair's biggest challenge. Some of the greatest battles between an offensive tackle and a defensive end I ever saw were between Bob and Gino. It was the battle of battles. Seeing them go after each other while watching the game films was unbelievable. You know, they played together at USF. We played them twice a year and Bob would maybe dominate one game and Gino another. It was a big rivalry. It was really something to watch those guys go at each other. I have not seen a battle like that since.

R. C. Owens, 49er halfback also remembers the battles between Marchetti and St. Clair.

You talk about battles! These guys used to hook up like David and Goliath on the football field. To this day you don't know who won – it was such a scrimmage between those two. They had played college ball together so they already knew each other's moves pretty well. Greatness on how the game was played in the NFL was measured by those two guys.

The great Baltimore Colts' quarterback and teammate of Gino Marchetti, Johnny Unitas had this to say about the St. Clair-Marchetti match-ups.

117

Bob's pass blocking was invincible. It was only when St.

Clair faced Gino Marchetti that the odds came down to dead even.

The St. Clair-Marchetti war was every bit as earth shaking as the

Sam Huff-Jim Brown love match. I'm just glad I didn't have to play

against him!

Gino Marchetti is considered one of the best defensive ends that ever played the game. He and I were very good friends and teammates at the University of San Francisco. In the NFL we played opposite each other for 12 years; myself being an offensive right tackle and he being a defensive left end. And I can remember before the game we never even spoke...we tried not to look at each other. And when the game started (on the line) I would step back and he would try to get around me and I would leg whip him. I would immediately stand up, run back and help him up. He would brush me off, not talk to me. The other reason I did that was that I didn't want him to be pissed off at me cause then he would be even more difficult to block.

There were times on the line. Gino would say, 'Goddamn it Bob! You were holding me. I told the ref you were holding me'. I would say, 'It must have been an accident, Gino. It must have been an accident. My hand must have got caught'. After the game we would get together, go out to dinner and talk about old times and such. But boy, when that game started, only eye contact was made....otherwise I didn't look his way

Every once in a while Gino would take that outside rush. If he was fast enough and the inside rush by Artie Donovan or Big Daddy Lipscomb would break through, Tittle couldn't step forward. I would be thinking that Tittle was going to step up in the pocket but sometimes he wasn't able to. As I turned and looked back I would see what was happening. Tittle refers to it as *the lookout play*. I would turn with Gino at the same time and say, 'Look out Y! Look out!' And Tittle would duck or try to avoid him. That way he would know he was coming.

Defensive end, Dan Colchico is a great buddy of mine. He tells a pretty funny story about a game where one of our players found a way to get rid of Marchetti – legally!

Bob was banged up pretty good and we were playing against Baltimore – Marchetti – and there was always a battle between those two – some damn good battles. What the 49ers did was put in center, Frank Morze, who too, was a little banged up, at the OT position. And his job was to hold Marchetti. Marchetti hated to be held. Morze wasn't fast enough to stop my grandmother on the outside, but on the inside he was a great ball player, great center. So here he is against Marchetti and sure enough, he held him about three times in a row. Marchetti took a swing at Morze.

119

They were both kicked out of the game. No big deal because that's why he

(Morze) was put in. Bob went back in and played against some rookie. We

ended up winning the game.

NFL SCANDAL – THE FIX

Sportswriter Bob Carroll is well aware that pro football lives

in mortal fear of a fix scandal.

Any suggestion that a game might not be played on the up-

and-up causes nightmares of the whole edifice tumbling into the

same category as pro wrestling. But late in 1962 odious rumors

began swirling.

San Francisco offensive tackle Bob St. Clair was said to be

somehow keeping time with mob figures. Chicago Bears fullback

Rick Casares was said to be keeping bad company. And Colt's owner

Carroll Rosenbloom was suspected of placing bets. In early

January, news leaked to the press that George Halas had asked the

league to look into some things he'd heard involving 'a member of a

Midwestern team.'

On the afternoon of April 17, Commissioner Rozelle

announced he had suspended indefinitely two of the NFL's greatest

stars – 'Golden Boy' Paul Hornung of Green Bay and 'Bad Boy'

Alex Karras of Detroit – for betting on games. In the end the league's investigation cleared St. Clair, Casares and Rosenbloom of any wrong doing.

In early 1962, I received a call from the Senate Rackets Committee – they had subpoenaed me. I was gong to have to testify as far as gambling in the NFL. There were four of us: Alex Karras, Paul Horning and Rick Casares. We all got called in. I immediately called my buddy, Pete Rozelle. I told him that this was a bunch of bologna…and to call off the wolves and intervene in my behalf. He said, 'Bob, we can't. We can't even get close to this. It's an image thing dealing with gambling in the NFL. I recommend you get an attorney real fast.' I did. There was only one consultation with this attorney. He said. 'Whatever they say, you answer NO to everything.'

When I was being questioned in the courtroom, they clicked a picture of this guy on a screen on the wall. They asked me if I knew this guy. 'Yeah, I know him. He's in the real estate business in South San Francisco. ' The prosecutor asked, 'Is he a friend of yours?' 'Yeah I go to his house for barbeques and stuff like that. He's been very active in politics over the last two years.' And then they showed the next picture of him with holding a number underneath when they had booked him in the 1940's for bookmaking.

'Did you have conversations with him in regard to betting on games?' I said, 'No. I never had any conversations. I don't bet on football. I don't bet on games. I just don't bet, period.' They continued to ask me about trivial things on betting – like the cards. I continued to say NO to everything they asked. Then they asked Karras and Horning the same questions. Paul had told me later that he said, 'Yeah, I bet those cards every week. They're just 'fun things'. And if I know we are going to beat a certain team badly I bet on our team.' Alex Karras was also involved. Rick Casaras had said the same thing I said...No, No. No. Horning and Karras both were suspended without pay for one year from the League. Naturally the papers were all over it that I was 'guilty by association'. But after the league's investigation had been completed Casares and myself were cleared.

HOLLYWOOD CALLS FOR TARZAN

Bruno Banducci, a terrific offensive guard for the 49ers, gave me the nickname *The Geek*. It came from that old movie where Tyrone Power would eat live chickens in a carnival sideshow. I don't eat chickens like that. The feathers, you know. But I like them rare.

I'll leave the sideshows to Tyrone Power, but I nearly got into the movies. This was back when I was still playing. Johnny Weissmuller had just retired, and they were looking for a Tarzan. Walt Daley, a sportswriter out here, thought of the idea and acted as my agent. He called down to Paramount Studios and asked them if they were still looking for a Tarzan. He tells them about my playing and some of my habits – the raw meat, etc. – so they ask me to come down for an interview.

I went down and actually went through an audition. I read lines, went out on the back lot and climbed a rope hand-over-hand, swung from platform to platform, dove into a water tank and they took some water shots of me with a knife in my mouth. Walt Daley was very optimistic. He thought we were really going to do this.

The only thing was, that they had me running into a bamboo-walled village and confronting these savages. Well, all these guys were about five feet seven. I'm six nine. I looked like I was Gulliver! I didn't know if they were going to throw ropes over me or what. The movie people were going to build a trench for me to run around in so that I would look small with all these short guys. Kind of the opposite of those ramps they used to have Alan Ladd walk on so he'd look taller. Well, it ended up that the part went to a Hollywood guy by the name of Ron Ely. I was just too tall.

THE BREWERY

It seems unthinkable now, but most players in the early fifties still required regular jobs in the off-season to support themselves.

When I first went to work for the Burgermeister brewery in 1954, Franklin Mieuli was my boss. He had worked out a deal with Burgermeister and the 49ers broadcasting setup.

Franklin hired me during the off-season. He was a department of one and with me; he was a department of two.

The brewery used to give us $150.00 in $2.00 bills. That was our trademark when we would travel to the distributors. In one week we would go from San Francisco to Bakersfield, to Fresno, to Sacramento to Modesto. How we would work this is to go to a distributor, in let's say, Fresno. He would give us a list of accounts (bars) that had dropped Burgi. Franklin and I would go to these bars around 8 or 9 in the morning and we would buy everyone drinks (including ourselves) using the $2.00 bills. I couldn't drink beer that early, so I would have orange juice and vodka because of the *healthy aspect* of it. Later that same day we would have lunch with one of the bar owners and begin drinking martinis. I was averaging about 25-30 drinks a day. There were times in the evening that I had to carry

Franklin from the car to the room. The next morning we would start

all over again. We did very well with those bars. We got the

accounts back and they all put Burgermeister beer back in their bars.

YOU KILLED MY STAR!

After our '57 year we had an off-season basketball team. We had

some real good players on the team: R. C. Owens, an All American out of

Idaho @ Boise, Clyde Connors was All Coast, Billy Wilson was an

outstanding player out of San Jose State and Gordy Soltau who was another

great player. I played center. We would use Tittle or McElhenny as

window dressing because of their name. Mac could dribble a lot - he was a

good dribbler, but that was the extent of it. He wasn't an ace at scoring.

After the '57 year we had some real good offers to play. At first

we were playing just Northern California…Bakersfield, Fresno, Sacramento

and Vallejo. One day we received a call from Abe Saperstein, the owner of

the Harlem Globe Trotters. The Globe Trotters were playing at the Cow

Palace in San Francisco. He asked us if we would consider playing them.

We told him yes. Usually we would get fifty dollars a piece per game, but

the deal was that we would be guaranteed two-hundred dollars a piece.

Gordy Soltau made a deal that if there were a certain amount of people at the Cow Palace that we would get additional compensation. But what happened is that the Cow Palace sold out! There were sixteen thousand people there! We made almost seven hundred dollars a piece. It was like we had died and gone to Heaven!

Just before the game Abe Saperstein came in and told us how the *game* would be played. It was basically choreographed. He asked who the center would be. I told him that I was. Then Saperstein told me, 'When Wilt comes along the key he will dribble in like he's going for the basket, step on the foul line and dunk the ball. Go along the side of him like you are going to guard him.'

First quarter, here comes Wilt. He comes flying around the corner of the key, plants his foot and as he goes up for the basket he backhands an elbow at me and almost knocks me down. As he scored, I made the comment to him, 'Don't do that again.' He made some remark like, 'Sure, just stay out of my way.'

As the game progressed, he did it again. This time I was ready for him and I put up my guard. After he had made the shot I stepped in front of him and said, 'I told you not to do that again, because if you do it again, god damnit, you're goin' down!' 'Yeah, sure, St. Clair.' said Chamberlain.

Third quarter, same thing he comes around the key. Instead of moving sideways, I stepped in front of him and as he starts going towards

126

me – trying to hit me with that elbow - I head butt him right in the chest, knock him upside down in the air and the first thing that hits the floor is the back of his head. He's lying there on the ground and I'm yelling at him, 'God damnit, I told you not to do that. Get up you son of a bitch! Get up!! I'll kill you!'

Abe Saperstein came running off the bench yelling at me, 'Are you crazy! This is my star! You killed him!' I said, 'I told that son of a bitch not to do that again and he did it!' The fans were going crazy. They thought it was part of the act. They were yelling and screaming. From that time forward, Wilt and I became real good friends. We later toured Canada and played four games together. I made some real good money. Far more than I ever did playing football.

ST. CLAIR HANGS IT UP

In 1962 St. Clair lost most of the season due to an Achilles tendon tear. He returned to the 49ers the following season. Not only was he voted by his teammates to receive the prestigious Len Eshmont Inspirational Player award, but he was also selected to the All Pro team.

However prior to the '64 season Bob ruptured the Achilles tendon in his other heel during an exhibition game and was forced to retire from football. His entire 12-year career, from 1953-1964 was with the 49ers. All-NFL three times, he also started in five Pro Bowls. He was as colorful and versatile on the field as off the field.

Although the 49ers failed to win a championship during the decade of the 50's, they continued to thrill us with exciting, unforgettable games and great leading characters. Men like St. Clair, Tittle, McElhenny and Perry still symbolize the glamour and glory of the game.

Detroit Lion quarterback and Hall of Fame member Bobby Layne was a good friend of mine. He was one of the most outlandish players in the history of the NFL – but he was also one of the best. Bobby loved the game as much as he loved his teammates. This is what he said after retiring from the game. He hit it right on the head.

I'll tell you what I really miss. What I miss are the guys. That's what I miss more than anything. I miss going to training camp. I miss the road trips and the card games. I miss the fellowship. The locker room, the places where it was a pleasure to be. The practice sessions. I miss the bar where we'd go for a beer after practice. I miss having that beer with the guys. I miss the ball games. I mean, when you've got a whole team looking forward to everything, when you've got guys showing up for practice early and staying late – well, you've got something there. We had that perfect

thing for a while. What I miss now are my teammates.

I couldn't agree more with Bobby. It didn't get any better

than this.

Bob's 'life after football' was equally as colorful as it was

distinctive. A mayor, a county supervisor, a lobbyist and dining with

JFK, a field to call his own and a jersey retirement that was long

overdue.

NATIONAL FOOTBALL LEAGUE
STANDARD PLAYERS CONTRACT

BETWEEN

Anthony J. Morabito and Victor P. Morabito (A Limited Partnership)

which operates San Francisco Forty-Niners

and which is a member of the National Football

League and which is hereinafter called the "Club," and Robert B. St. Clair of

Tulsa, Oklahoma

hereinafter called the "Player."

In consideration of the respective promises herein, the parties hereto agree as follows:

Bob's first contract—$6000—1953

Signing autographs in the
Kezar parking lot after a game

J.D. Smith and Bob in the showers after a game

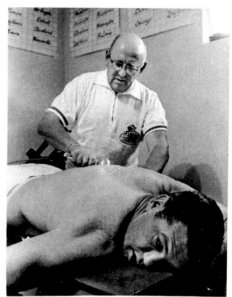

Bob with trainer Henry Schmidt

Ted Connolly, Matt Hazeltine, Tommy McCormick and Bob

In Hollywood with Alan Ameche (of the Colts), Bob, Jane Russell, Hugh Mc Elhenny and Billy Wilson

49ers vs. Redskins. Bob is #79.
Matt Hazeltine is #55

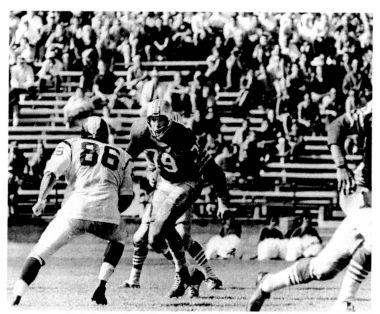

Bob faces Gene Brito #86 against the Redskins

Hugh McElhenny, #39, and Bob, #79, at rushing down field

49ers vs. Colts : future Hall of Fame members Hugh McElhenny,
Joe Perry, Gino Marchetti, Bob, Art Donovan

Blocking a punt against the Colts

Bob gives Y.A. Tittle the game ball

Bob is sidelined with an injury in the early 1960's

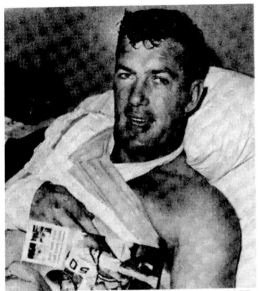

Hospitalized with a separated shoulder in 1957

In Honolulu for the 1957 Hula Bowl.
Players and wives at dinner

They played the Harlem Globetrotters:
Billy Wilson (84), Bob (79), Y.A. Tittle
(44), Don Burke (66), Gordy Soltau (82),
Hardy Brown (32)

Bob and family in the early 1960's

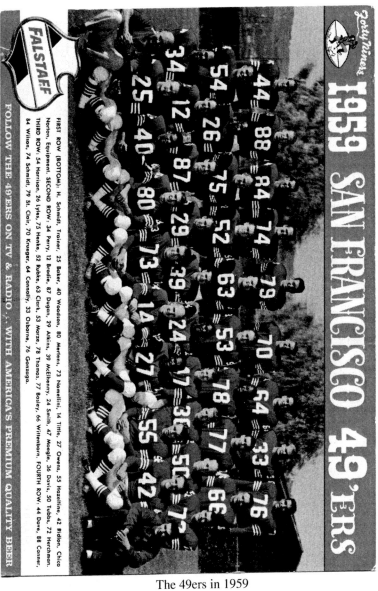

1959 SAN FRANCISCO 49'ERS

FIRST ROW (BOTTOM): H. Schmidt, Trainer, 25 Baker, 40 Woodson, 80 Merten, 73 Nomellini, 14 Tittle, 27 Owens, 55 Hazeltine, 42 Ridlon, Chico Norton, Equipment. SECOND ROW: 34 Perry, 12 Brodie, 87 Dugan, 29 Atkins, 39 McElhenny, 24 Smith, 47 Moegle, 36 Davis, 50 Tubbs, 72 Herchman. THIRD ROW: 54 Harrison, 26 Lyles, 75 Henke, 52 Rubke, 63 Clark, 53 Morze, 78 Thomas, 77 Bosley, 66 Wittenborn. FOURTH ROW: 44 Dove, 88 Conner, 84 Wilson, 74 Schmidt, 79 St. Clair, 70 Krueger, 64 Connolly, 33 Osborne, 76 Gonzaga.

The 49ers in 1959

FOURTH QUARTER

Life After Football – A Field of Dreams

The field at Kezar became
Bob St. Clair Field in 2001

*S*t. Clair's political career began while he was still with the 49ers. He was elected City Councilman of Daly City, California in 1958 at the age of 27. Joe Verducci, Bob's former high school coach and himself, a former mayor, served with Bob on the City Council.

At age 30 he was appointed Mayor of Daly City. Later he also served as Chairman of the Board of Supervisors, San Mateo County. His role in seeking integrated housing caught the attention of JFK. St. Clair was particularly active in Kennedy's presidential campaign in 1960 and was later invited to the White House.

He ended his political career in Sacramento as a Lobbyist for Orange County, California.

YOU LEGISLATE LIKE YOU PLAY!

When I was the mayor of Daly City I was also captain of the 49ers. The team wasn't doing so well that particular season. At that time I ran my council meetings on Monday night – the day after our game at Kezar. Depending on how well or how poorly we played alerted me as to what kind of reaction I should expect from the audience.

141

I distinctly remember one such hearing very well. At that time, Highway 280 was in the process of being built and the state began confiscating property. The farmers who owned that property were not happy with the fact that they would be coming through their fields and taking over.

One of our meetings was held the night after we had lost a game and really played poorly. I was running the meeting. The council and myself had voted to go along with one of the state issues regarding the passage of Highway 280. The majority of the farmers in the audience didn't like the way we voted. They began yelling and screaming. I kept hitting the gavel to quiet them down. Finally one of the Italian farmers got up and in broken English said, 'Bob a St. a Clair! You a legislate like a you play a the football on Sunday....the shits!' I banged the gavel and told the bailiff to get him out of here!

Bob had one tremendous advantage over other Mayors. Nobody – but nobody – ever dreamed of fighting HIS City Hall...with one minor exception!

After John Kennedy's election in 1960, St. Clair, also a Democrat, decided to put up a large picture of the new president in the Council chambers at City Hall. Instantly there arose a loud outcry; the Council is a nonpartisan body (Californians take their non-partisan politics very seriously). Mayor St. Clair ignored the objections and hung the portrait. He turned to his fellow councilmen and townspeople and said: 'He's the president of ALL the people, isn't he?' The council members quickly shut up.

KENNEDY AND THE WHITE HOUSE

When I was playing with the 49ers, Paul 'Red' Fay was a 49er fan. Red was in the Navy with Jack Kennedy when he captained the PT 109.

In 1960, Fay (who was one of JFK's campaign managers and a close friend) and I worked on Kennedy's presidential campaign. As a matter of fact, Ted Kennedy would come out to San Francisco and we would go out at night and drink. We both were pretty young then. I was also the Northern California Chairman for 'Athletes for Kennedy' (the Southern California Chairman was Rosie Grier from the Rams).

After the election was over and Kennedy had won, Jack made Red Fay one of his Under Secretaries of the Navy.

In 1962, when we were going back to play Baltimore, I got a call from Red and he said 'Bob why don't you come by the White House. Jack would like to meet with you. I'll send a car.'

When I arrived in Baltimore I was picked up in a limo. The car had the presidential seal and all the flags. They brought me over to the White House and I met with the President. He was talking to me about football. He loved football. He was naming players and asking me about this guy and that guy. But we were constantly being interrupted by people coming in who needed to speak with the President. Finally Jack said, 'Bob, I've just been informed that we have a problem. I have to meet with my advisors to see if we can solve it. I'm very sorry. Maybe we can do this again.' And he left.

I was driven back to the hotel. I later found out that the problem had to do with a Russian ship. It was the beginning of the Bay of Pigs. The biggest problem I had was that we lost the game against Baltimore.

CHAIRMAN OF THE BOARD OF SUPERVISORS
THE SAN GREGORIO NUDE BEACH

When I was the Chairman of the Board of Supervisors in San Mateo County back in 1970, we held our meetings at the County

144

Center in Redwood City. Near the end of these meetings we would allow time for comments by the audience. One time we had this woman complaining about the beach at San Gregorio. She and her two young daughters were walking along San Gregorio beach when all of a sudden they came face to face with two nude people. She was complaining that something had to be done about the nudists. I suggested that I make a field trip out there and investigate. The board looked at me kind of strange but agreed to it.

The following Sunday afternoon I was picked up by helicopter from Coyote Point and was taken up the coast to San Gregorio beach. As we flew over San Gregorio beach I could see that there were at least 300 people or more….and they were all nude – no clothes on! They were all ages, all sizes, all shapes and all colors. Some were playing Frisbee – some were playing volleyball…..just bouncing around having a good time.

The sheriff's helicopter was all green with two big stars and red lights. I told the pilot to fly over the people and announce to them that this was the Sheriff's department and that we would be landing. We landed in the middle of the beach and I got out. All these people ran up to me….everyone of them was nude. You know it's very difficult to talk to people when you have clothes on and they don't.

I asked who the spokesperson was for this group. I told them that this was an illegal action. As they began talking amongst themselves my head was going back and forth. Finally I said, 'Why don't you all form a circle. I will stand in the middle and we can talk.'

I began the meeting with all these people around me. To try and talk and have eye-to-eye contact with people when they don't have clothes on was pretty strange. There they were – men and women sitting on the sand with their legs apart. It was very distracting.

I finally told them that we couldn't have this kind of activity on a public beach. 'What I am going to do is recommend to the Board that we put a sign up on each end of the beach saying WARNING: You Are Entering a Clothes-Optional Beach. This will at least warn the others.'

I went back to the Board and told them what I had suggested about the sign. We had all men and one woman on the Board. Naturally, all of the men were asking me question. 'Hey, Bob, did you join in their festivities? You kept your clothes on...we assume?

THE HALL OF FAME CALLS...FINALLY

Bob St. Clair was accorded pro football's highest honor on August 4, 1990. His induction into the Pro Football Hall of Fame came almost 27 years after he threw his last block on an NFL gridiron. St. Clair, the senior nominee, spent his entire 12-year career with the 49ers from 1953 to1964.

All NFL three times, he also started in five Pro Bowls. Additionally Bob was named to the *Team of the Decade* along with 49er teammates – Hugh McElhenny, Joe Perry and Leo Nomellini; and along with USF teammates, Dick Stanfel, Ollie Matson and Gino Marchetti.

ACCOLADES FROM TEAMMATES, FRIENDS AND COLLEAGUES

In the 12-year period from 1953 to 1964, St. Clair provided protection for some of history's finest backs - Y. A. Tittle, Joe Perry, John Henry Johnson and Hugh McElhenny. All four members of that 'Million Dollar Backfield' are now in the Pro Football Hall of Fame. So it is only fitting that St. Clair, whose blocks undoubtedly hastened

the foursome's march to the Hall, is in the Hall of Fame as well. –
Pro Football Hall of Fame

Bob St. Clair, semi-seriously stated he didn't like being called an 'old timer.' Considering the fact that St. Clair is 6'9' and eats raw meat, it didn't take long for the Hall of Fame to start using the 'politically correct' term 'Senior'. - *Rusty Miller/Associated Press Writer*

I played in several Pro Bowls with Bob and I could never understand his lack of recognition. Watching films, I saw him cut defenders in half with his blocks. – *Jim Ringo/Green Bay Packers* – *Pro Football Hall of Fame*

He was an outstanding offensive tackle. There was no doubt he helped make my career successful. – *John Henry Johnson/San Francisco 49ers* – *Pro Football Hall of Fame*

Some say St. Clair lacked the recognition he deserved because he never compiled the statistics the 'Million Dollar Backfield' did. But St. Clair said statistics in his day were insignificant. – Mike Popovich/Canton Repository sportswriter

There was no question I thought he would eventually get into the Hall of Fame. I knew his day would finally come. – Hugh McElhenny/San Francisco 49ers – Pro Football Hall of Fame

There is something about St. Clair that epitomizes professional football. He was good and more to the point, he was mean. In brief, Bob St. Clair is the player who substantiates the argument that football players were tougher 40 years ago. In 1990 St. Clair's greatness was belatedly recognized when he was enshrined in the Pro Football Hall of Fame. – Bob Carroll/sportswriter

I' feel that the Hall of Fame voters of today cannot determine what great play was in the 50's. The game was different; the rules for the offensive tackle were different. How Bob performed and what he accomplished was beyond the means of what an offensive tackle was supposed to do. He was ahead of his time. – R. C. Owens/San Francisco 49ers

Each year the Hall of Fame brings in old timers to talk about the old timers they played against. Jim Ringo and I were brought in to Canton to meet with sportswriters about who should be the old timer selected to the Hall.

They gave us orders to rate them from 1-10. 10 being the best you could get. They presented us with this whole list of names. Bob was one of the names. When I saw his name I said, 'Don't even ask me because he is better than a 10.' And that was true. I was glad that the sportswriters listened to us. That's the way it should be.

- Sam Huff/New York Giants, Pro Football Hall of Fame

Bob was a great player and deserved to be in the Hall of Fame way before this. One of his teammates, Billy Kilmer, was so upset that he wasn't in the Hall twenty years ago that he took on a personal crusade to do what he had to do to get Bob the recognition that he deserved. – George Blanda/Chicago Bears/Oakland Raiders, Pro Football Hall of Fame

I remember the end of the 80's when he didn't get into the Hall of Fame. I used to get on people all the time. I said if you don't get Bob St. Clair into the Hall of Fame the Hall of Fame has no credibility. I don't know how much good it did but I told Bart Starr

150

and some of the Player's Committee that you gotta get Bob in the HOF because there was nobody better than him in that position. – Billy Kilmer/San Francisco 49ers

I always said he was the best. He was so tall that he could cut you down with his legs. And he was pretty good at it. The passing game wasn't emphasized that much so he could pass block and run block. Linemen were basically run blockers. He was a hell of a football player. And I have great respect for him as a person because he handles himself so well. – Mike Ditka/Chicago Bears, Pro Football Hall of Fame

He was a great football player. He deserves all the honors and accolades that he has received. – Billy Wilson/San Francisco 49ers

Within the confines of world famous Golden Gate Park, Kezar Stadium was dedicated to the City of San Francisco in 1925. St. Clair's entire high school, college and pro career were played on this home field – an unprecedented 189 games – more than anyone else in the history of Kezar Stadium.

A FIELD TO CALL HIS OWN

Charles McDermid, sportswriter for the San Francisco Examiner wrote this about Bob upon hearing that the field at Kezar Stadium would be named Bob St. Clair Field.

With the grace belying his 69 years, St. Clair strolled into Kezar Stadium on Thursday, just minutes after the San Francisco Park and Recreation Board Commission voted unanimously to rename the field Bob St. Clair Field in his honor.

St. Clair was the natural choice as the field's patron. Beginning with his days as a star athlete at now-closed Polytechnic High School, which stood directly across the street, and extending though his eleven years with the 49ers, St. Clair played 17 seasons and 189 games on the grass at Kezar Stadium

Bob's first response to hearing about the field was 'unbelievable'.

It's a done deal now. I'm still on cloud nine. Come on, if you're born and raised in San Francisco, and were fortunate enough to have the talent to make the Pro Football Hall of Fame, then find out that they named a field where you played after you - how fortunate can a person be? It's mind-boggling.

I can still hear the crowd. We loved playing here. When it had rained, the field was the muddiest thing you ever saw. I can remember being here covered in mud and blood, the crowd cheering.

Today at the Board meeting, one of the members said he used to come watch me play from the Christopher Milk section when he was young. That's what everyone says now, 'I saw you play when I was young. 'That'll make you feel pretty old.

When I go out and give talks to different organizations, (St. Clair now works in sales and public relations for Clover-Stornetta Farms) I always mention how proud I am to have played more games at Kezar than anyone.

Unbeknownst to me, Kristine Clark, who is writing a book on the undefeated USF team I was on in 1951, was also authoring a proposal to the Park and Recreation Commission. She campaigned, with the help of my daughter Lynn, (behind my back) to have the field named after me. When I got word that the Park and Recreation Commission had voted unanimously to do that, I thought, 'C'mon. No Way'. I just flipped. I'm still overwhelmed. Talk about being blessed as an athlete...I feel like Joe DiMaggio.

I thought being enshrined in the Pro Football Hall of Fame was the ultimate, but this idea of having the field where you played all your home games named after you, well, that takes the cake.

His legacy in place, St. Clair was asked how he would like to be remembered by those who see his name on the field at Kezar Stadium.

For football, what else?

On January 19th, 2001, the field at Kezar Stadium was named Bob St. Clair Field. That I was instrumental in the City of San Francisco according him this honor makes me humble but proud.

So on this day, his playing career – Poly, USF, the 49ers – comes full circle. The following is the dedication speech I gave in honor of Bob St. Clair Field.

Kristine Clark/Author

We all have heroes. Mine was Bob St. Clair.

In 1958 I attended my first professional football game at Kezar Stadium. The Green Bay Packers were playing the San Francisco 49ers. My dad was a season ticket holder. We sat in the 66th row....the very top of the stadium on a crowded, backless bench. This was when Kezar held 60,000 people. The steps to the top seemed to be never-ending My dad always loved those seats. I can remember him saying, 'You can see the entire field from up here, you can lean back against the wall and there's no one behind you if you want to stand up.' All I knew is that it was cold and windy and the players looked like ants.

When I complained about not being able to see very well, my dad would give me his binoculars. He told me to keep them focused on the tunnel because the players would soon be coming out of there. I did just that.

Moments later the announcer came over the loud speaker and began introducing the 49ers. As their names were called, they ran out of the tunnel one by one. The roar of the crowd became thunderous - almost frightening.

The names of these gridiron warriors were not new to me. They were as common in my household as were those of my family. Tittle, McElhenny, Perry, Nomelllini and Owens; or as they were more commonly known to the San Francisco fans as YAT, The King, The Jet, The Lion and the Alley Oop.

With the binoculars held firmly in my hands, I closely followed each and every one of them as they jogged out on to the *field and made their cut to the left which was simply known as the*

'49er side'.

As each player's name was announced, so was his height,

weight and position. That day, one player, in particular, stood out

among all the others. He was literally heads and shoulders above

the rest. His name was Bob St. Clair. I had heard his name

mentioned on radio and television many times before; and I

remember my dad talking about how at 6' 9' - 265 lbs, he was the

'biggest player in professional football' and one of the hardest

hitting.

Through the binoculars, I watched Bob run out of that

tunnel. He was bigger than life. I followed him as he made the cut

and then shook the hands of his fellow teammates. To say that I was

in awe of this man would have been an understatement.

With my father's permission I ran down the never-ending

flights of steps to the steel bars and railings below that separated the

fans from the field. I flung my legs through the lower bar and sat

down, resting my arms on the bar above. As I scanned the 49er

bench, I again found myself focused on St. Clair. But this time it was

something other than his size that caught my eye. It was his jersey.

His number was 79. My birthday was July 9th; 7-9. I thought that was pretty cool. Little did I know that this 'common bond' would come into play later on down the road.

At the end of the game, I had asked my dad if I could meet Bob and get his autograph. My dad being a typical 50's father responded in a sympathetic voice, 'The players don't want to be bothered at the end of the game. They are anxious to get home and be with their families.' Needless to say, I was extremely disappointed.

My dad worked for the San Francisco News-Call Bulletin - one of the three major newspapers in the City at that time. The following day, he brought a surprise home for me. He had obtained a publicity photo of Bob from the sports department. I ran into my room and taped it to my wall.

The picture somewhat lessened the disappointment of not meeting him that Sunday. And besides, there were still a few more home games left in the season - I would get a chance to meet him then. But fate didn't see it the same way. It wouldn't be until forty-one seasons later, and ironically at the age of 49, that I would finally be granted my wish.

My story begins several years ago. While working on my Doctorate degree at USF, a mysterious messenger left an NFL Films'

157

video on my desk. To this day I don't know who or why. I had no idea of the contents until I brought it home. Viewing it with my husband, Bill, he said, 'That's the 1951 University of San Francisco Dons football team. They had a phenomenal line up!' As we watched I couldn't believe my eyes. One of the players was my eighth grade typing teacher from A. P. Giannini Junior High School - Mr. Bill Henneberry, the other, my childhood football hero, Bob St. Clair.

I was immediately pulled in by this story and decided to research it further. I started with questions to the University's athletic director. He in turn pointed me in the direction of the Director of Athletic Development - who else, but Bill Henneberry. As we talked, a story line for a book was born. The title would be, 'Undefeated, Untied and Uninvited - The Story of the 1951 University of San Francisco Dons Football Team .'

Personal interviews with team members were key to the book, and I began scheduling them immediately. I scheduled my first interview with Bob.

The date was Saturday, January 22, 2000. We had decided to meet at a restaurant called The Nutty Irishman in Santa Rosa, California. Even though my anxiety level was at an all time high the interview went well. He eventually became my consultant to the book.

One day while driving by Kezar Stadium, I asked Bob if we could go in. Ever accommodating, he sort of hesitated, which was strange. But he finally agreed and we stopped. Just before getting out of the car, he again hesitated and said it was too cold. I said, 'Oh, c'mon.'

As we approached the Kezar arch, he stopped and slowly scanned the stadium as if it were the grand structure that it once was. I felt that in his mind he was seeing Kezar as it used to be. I took his arm and said, 'Come on, let's run on the field!' In a quiet voice he said, 'No, let's walk on the track.' I shrugged my shoulders and reluctantly, but silently agreed. As we walked towards the tunnel, his eyes continued to scan the stadium.

Standing in front of the tunnel's entrance, I commented on how dungeon-like it appeared. He responded with, 'It's exactly like it was when I played here.'

As I continued to peer into the darkness, I heard Bob say in a nostalgic tone, 'I can still hear the crowd.' Those of you who know Bob know that he can get a little theatrical at times, but this time it was no act. I turned to look at him and I immediately knew he was remembering the days when the crowds would hang over the

bleachers to watch and hopefully touch the players as they ran

through the tunnel. At this point I had stepped back and just watched

him.

He turned to me and said, 'I can still hear the announcers

as they called out our names; 'Tittle, McElhenny, Nomellini, 'St.

Clair.' Just then he dropped down into a three--point stance and as

if he were transformed back into that magical point in time, jogged

out onto the field and made a cut to the left to where the 49er bench

once stood. He stopped and turned around. He glanced at me and

then slowly scanned the stadium. 'God, I love this game and I love

this field', he said. I felt so very sad for him. He no longer was that

young man but for a fraction of time it was as if time had stood still;

to him the crowd's roar was only a moment ago.

As we walked back to the car, it was then that he told me

that he had played 189 games on this field - Polytechnic High

School, USF and the 49ers.

I went home and told my husband about the afternoon. He

was so intrigued by the story that he said, 'Someone who has played

that many home games on the same field should have that field

named after them. My response was, 'Why not?'

In August of 2000 I wrote a proposal to the San Francisco Park and Recreation Department requesting that the field at Kezar Stadium be named, 'Bob St. Clair Field'. On January 18th, 2001 the Park and Recreation Commission unanimously passed the proclamation naming the field within Kezar Stadium, Bob St. Clair Field. The rest is history.

One of the constants of American sports throughout the years has been football. Like baseball, it too, is a mark of time. This field, this game and this man are all a part of our past and for most of us here today, a part of our youth - but his legacy will live on as future generations of athletes continue to do battle on a gridiron simply known as St. Clair Field.

For 18 seasons Bob called Kezar Stadium, home, and now, 37 years after playing his final professional game in this ballpark, he has returned to claim this field of dreams as his own.

On a personal note: Thank you for resurrecting my youth and for all the wonderful and exciting memories you have given to me.

Welcome home, Robert.

During my first interview with Bob I asked him what he considered to be the biggest disappointment of his career. Without hesitation he replied, *'They (the 49ers) never retired my jersey!'*

Collaborating with 49er CEO Peter Harris and head coach Steve Mariucci, Bob's disappointment would end at 3Com Park (formally Candlestick Park) on December 2, 2001. Kristine Clark/Author

THE 49ERS HANG IT UP

Matt Maiocco, sportswriter for the Santa Rosa Press Democrat newspaper wrote this about Bob after finding out about his jersey retirement.

Tackle Bob St. Clair was the first 49ers player to wear #79 when the joined the team in 1953.

In all, seven 49ers wore the jersey number. But after Sunday night, # 79 will belong forever to St. Clair .

The 49ers officially retired #79 in honor of St. Clair at halftime of the 49ers victory over the Buffalo Bills. St. Clair becomes the ninth player in 49er history to have his number retired. The others are quarterbacks John Brodie (#12) and Joe Montana (#16), running backs Joe Perry (#34) and Hugh McElhenny (#39), receiver

Dwight Clark (#87), tackle Leo Nomellini (#73), defensive tackle

Charlie Krueger (#70) and defensive back Jimmy Johnson (#37).

The other 49ers players to wear #79 after St. Clair retired

after the 1964 season were tackle Cas Banaszek ('67-'77), defensive

ends Al Cowlings ('79), Jim Stuckey ('80-'85) and Glen Collins ('87)

and tackles Harris Barton ('87-'98) and Dan Dercher '(99-'00).

Many great players have worn the 49ers colors in the

team's fifty-plus years. But few can proudly say they're natives of

San Francisco. St. Clair, who graduated from Polytechnic High

School (which, Ironically, was located across the street from Kezar

Stadium), is one of the few.

'Sure, I love the City. This is my town,' St. Clair said.

The City and people of the region where he acceded to

Mayor of Daly City have returned the love. Their ultimate tribute

was naming the field at Kezar in his honor. They've never wondered

why there's a 'Saint' in his name.

OVERTIME – THE CHANGING FACE OF FOOTBALL

Before the paycheck was king, before astroturf, a flag for 'roughing the kicker' and instant replays, football was considered a 'true renegade's sport'. There was no need for an 'All Madden

Team' because everybody played with an intense desire solely for the love of the game. It was a time of innocence and greatness and the players were looked upon as *real* heroes.

Fred Dryer a defensive lineman who played with the Los Angeles Rams from 1972 through 1981 hit the nail on the head when he discussed the problem with today's players.

The problem with the players today isn't their talent, ability or intentions, but the fact that the National Football League lost control of the league in the ability to parent the players and coaches when they sold their rights to television. They gave up all their rights of standards of decency of sportsmanship to television. So the ownership and the coaches have no say so as to what the players say or do. It's the salary structure.

When Gene Upshaw put a hard cap on salaries, it separated the players in the locker room. You had a few players making a lot of money and you had the rest of the players playing for whatever they could get. At any point in time they could get axed. And they could come to you and say we need your money and you're to pay him and if you don't like it, we'll see ya. That's not right. What you get out of that are players who realize that they are not responsible for their actions.

It's simple. Bad behavior is bad behavior. The player who pulls an ink pen out and signs a football or the player who says, 'I'm not going to play my best today' is going to be taken outside and pounded by about five guys. I've seen it done before. It's a 'team' sport. Treat it as such!'

Money has changed the development of the game. When you go into battle you have to go into battle as a unit...as a team. If I don't know you then how can I go to the wall for you? I have to know something about you.

We have the problems that we do today because of the huge salaries. The guys now are not thinking about the pain and suffering that goes with the game. That used to be the beauty of playing the sport. How much pain you could take determined how tough you were. That was a big part of this game. – Deacon Jones/Los Angeles Rams, Pro Football Hall of Fame

Do you realize how much it would cost to get four guys of that caliber (such as the fearsome foursome) on the same team at the same time! Free agency breaks that all up. When I was playing for Green Bay, we had to stay with the same team. The camaraderie, the love that our teammates had for one another lasted throughout all these years. That's very, very important to a team. And that is one of the reasons why the Packers were so successful in the '60's. That's why there were dynasties. – Paul Hornung/Green Bay Packers, Pro Football Hall of Fame

It is still a great game. It is still America's game. No one can play it like we play it. But I think the rule makers have got to take a look at what has happened. Have they made the game better or have they hurt it. In my opinion, they have hurt it. – Sam Huff/New York Giants, Pro Football Hall of Fame

Real good life – hard life sometimes, but it's not supposed to be easy all your life. You are supposed to have some hardships. It makes you appreciate it when you get something. – Sammy Baugh/Washington Redskins, Pro Football Hall of Fame

Just being a part of the growth of the National Football League to me is the greatest thrill or event of my life. – George Halas/Founder, Owner and Coach of the Chicago Bears, Pro Football Hall of Fame

You look back at your football career and, of course, you adore it mainly because of the people you met and the men that you played with. – Red Grange/Chicago Bears, Pro Football Hall of Fame (Charter Enshrinee)

When discussing the game and the players of today, I think that Bob says it best:

I get questions all the time from people wondering how my era would have fared in today's era. Well let's look at it this way. I played both offense and defense predominately the whole game. We didn't have facemasks the first three years, our helmets were leather and we had numerous injuries where we had to play through. Now, I don't think the question should be whether or not we could play in today's league. I think the question should be, whether or not these 'candy asses' of today could play with us!

How true!

Today Bob lives in Santa Rosa, California with his wife Marsha. He is the father of six children, seventeen grandchildren and seven great-grandchildren.

His Honor the Mayor of Daly City, California, with
City Manager Ed Frank and Vice Mayor Joe Verducci 1958

Joe Louis, ex boxing heavyweight champion, Dan Galvin,
March of Dimes Chairman for Santa Rosa, CA, and Bob in 1959

Candidate for

County Supervisor
Robert "Bob"
ST. CLAIR
**A GOOD SUPERVISOR
KEEP HIM ON THE JOB!**

Election—Tues., June 4, 1974

Advance Print Shop, 264 Lorton, Burlingame, CA 94010

County Supervisor 1974

State Senate 1976

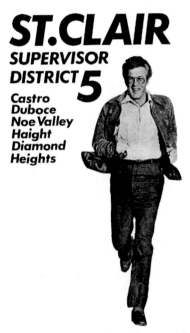

ST.CLAIR
SUPERVISOR
DISTRICT 5

Castro
Duboce
Noe Valley
Haight
Diamond
Heights

Running for San Francisco Board of Supervisors 1978

Bob with Jack Kemp in Washington D.C.

171

San Francisco mayor Joe Alioto, President Richard Nixon,
Cyril Magnin and Bob in 1973

Bob with First Lady Barbara Bush, President
George Bush with Bob's wife Marsha 1991

San Francisco 49er Legends
Hall of Fame Athletes

1990 Hall of Fame Inductees: Jack Lambert, Bob, Tom Landry, Bob Griese, Ted Hendricks, Buck Buchanan, Franco Harris

Hall of Fame induction speech 1990

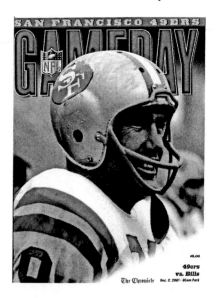

#79 jersey retirement at 3Com Park
December 2, 2001

Bob speaks at his jersey retirement ceremony 2001

Bob with Rosemary and 95 year old mother Agnes
(in the wheelchair) 2001

49er CEO Peter Harris and Head Coach Steve Mariucci at the
ceremony to name the field at Kezar Bob St. Clair Field 2001

The St. Clair family at Bob St. Clair Field (with Agnes in the
wheelchair) 2001

Bob with 49er greats John Henry Johnson, Y.A. Tittle, Charley
Kruger, Joe Perry and the plaque at Bob St. Clair Field

Bob with Y.A. Tittle, Joe Perry, and Dan Colchico at Bob St. Clair
Field

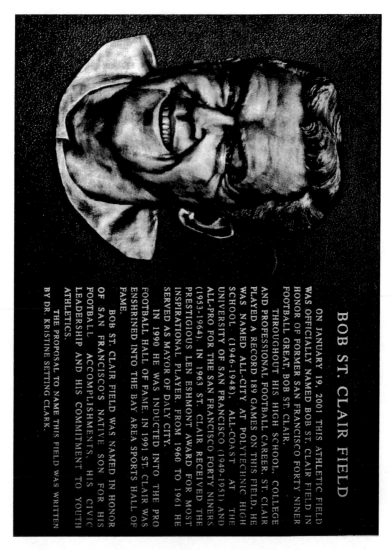

BOB ST. CLAIR FIELD

ON JANUARY 19, 2001 THIS ATHLETIC FIELD WAS OFFICIALLY NAMED BOB ST. CLAIR FIELD IN HONOR OF FORMER SAN FRANCISCO FORTY NINER FOOTBALL GREAT, BOB ST. CLAIR.

THROUGHOUT HIS HIGH SCHOOL, COLLEGE AND PROFESSIONAL FOOTBALL CAREER, ST. CLAIR PLAYED A RECORD 189 GAMES ON THIS FIELD. HE WAS NAMED ALL-CITY AT POLYTECHNIC HIGH SCHOOL (1946-1948). ALL-COAST AT THE UNIVERSITY OF SAN FRANCISCO (1949-1951) AND ALL-PRO FOR THE SAN FRANCISCO FORTY NINERS (1953-1964). IN 1963 ST. CLAIR RECEIVED THE PRESTIGIOUS LEN ESHMONT AWARD FOR MOST INSPIRATIONAL PLAYER. FROM 1960 TO 1961 HE SERVED AS MAYOR OF DALY CITY.

IN 1990 HE WAS INDUCTED INTO THE PRO FOOTBALL HALL OF FAME. IN 1991 ST. CLAIR WAS ENSHRINED INTO THE BAY AREA SPORTS HALL OF FAME.

BOB ST. CLAIR FIELD WAS NAMED IN HONOR OF SAN FRANCISCO'S NATIVE SON FOR HIS FOOTBALL ACCOMPLISHMENTS, HIS CIVIC LEADERSHIP AND HIS COMMITMENT TO YOUTH ATHLETICS.

THE PROPOSAL TO NAME THIS FIELD WAS WRITTEN BY DR. KRISTINE SETTING CLARK.

The plaque at Bob St. Clair Field, Kezar
Stadium, San Francisco, California

Author Kristine Clark with Bob St. Clair at
49er Fan Day at Kezar Stadium, Bob St. Clair Field
August 25, 2003